THE LIFE AND WORKS OF
FRANK LLOYD
WRIGHT

THE LIFE AND WORKS OF
FRANK LLOYD WRIGHT

Maria Costantino

Photography by
Simon Clay

COURAGE
BOOKS

AN IMPRINT OF RUNNING PRESS
PHILADELPHIA • LONDON

Copyright © 1998 PRC Publishing Ltd

First published in the United States in 1998 by
Courage Books

Printed and bound in China

9 8 7 6 5 4 3 2 1
Digit on the right indicates the number of this printing

Library of Congress Cataloging-in-Publication Number
97-77958

ISBN 0-7624-0378-0

First published in 1998 by
PRC Publishing Ltd, Kiln House, 210 New Kings Road,
London SW6 4NZ

Published by Courage Books, an imprint of
Running Press Book Publishers
125 South Twenty-second Street
Philadelphia, Pennsylvania 19103-4399

All photographs were taken by Simon Clay except
those on the following pages:
UPI/Bettman Newsphotos, 8,11,13,16,17
Frank Lloyd Wright Home and Studio Foundation, 9,
    10(TL)
© Hedrich Blessing/photo by Jon Miller, 10(BR)
© Pedro E. Guerroro, 14
© Ezra Stoller, ESTO Photographics
Barnaby's Picture Library, 20
Bison Picture Library, 23, 34
21, 22, 24, 25, 26, 27, 29, 30
Rijksmuseum Vincent Van Gogh, Amsterdam, 31(T)
Freer Gallery of Art, Smithsonian, Washington, DC,
    31(B)
Fallingwater, 92, 103

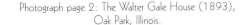

Photograph page 2: The Walter Gale House (1893),
Oak Park, Illinois.

Right: Anderton Court Center (1950), Beverly Hills, California.

CONTENTS

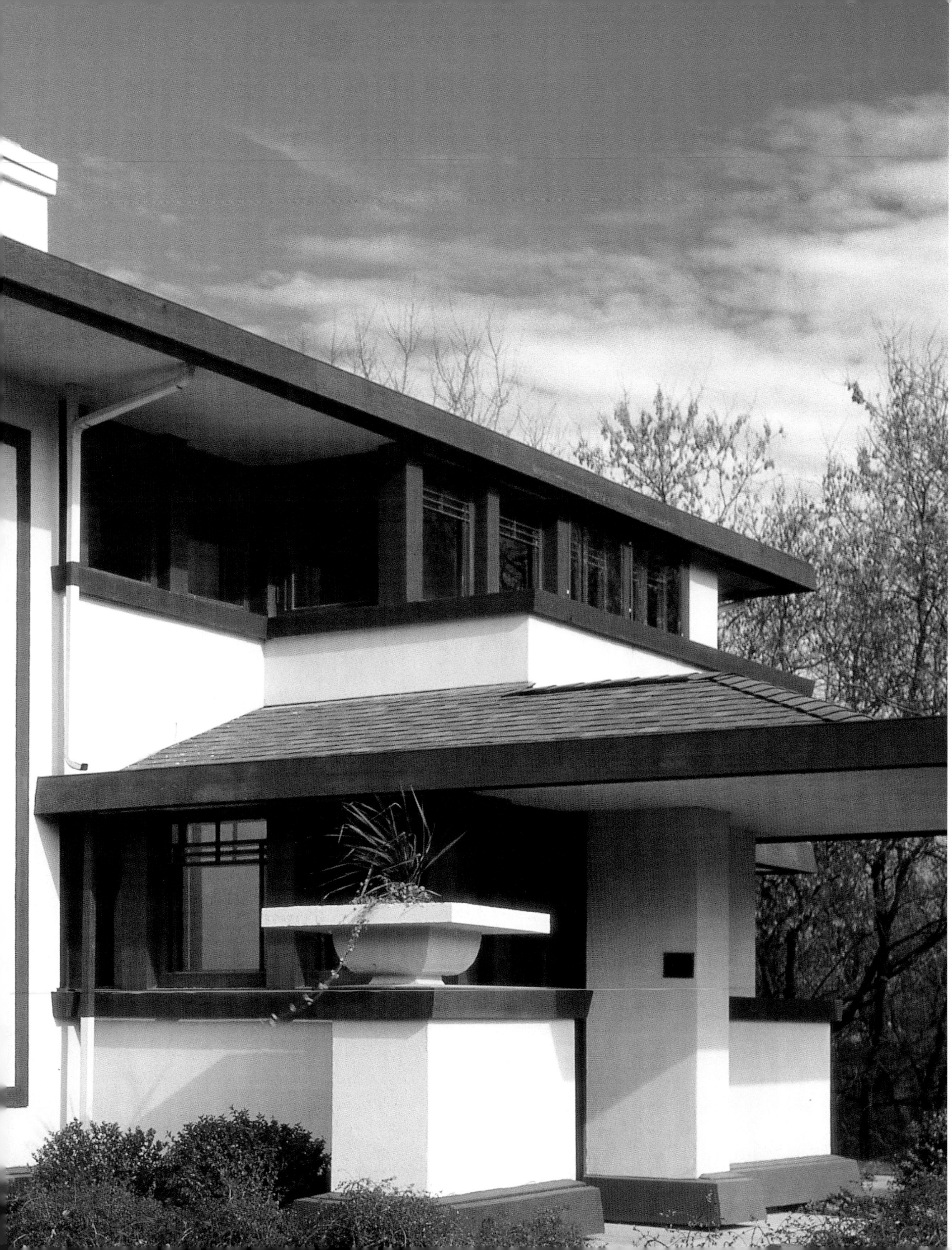

A PERSONAL PROFILE

A PERSONAL PROFILE

Frank Lloyd Wright has often been described as the greatest American architect. This opinion is one that Wright himself shared and was at pains to promote. His objection would have been that the use of the adjective "American" lessened his stature: while proud of his nation and his nationality, Wright's ego demanded that his contribution to the architecture of the 20th century be seen on a global scale! That he was a great architect was beyond doubt. This profession and his status within it, if we are to believe his autobiography which is full of inventions and versions of the truth, was chosen by his mother. Less well known than Frank Lloyd Wright architect and genius, is Frank Lloyd Wright the egocentric spendthrift, the womanizer, and the provider of many buildings with bulging walls and leaky roofs!

He was born—according to official records, that is—on June 8, 1867, in Richland Center, Wisconsin, a prosperous market town a few miles north of Spring Green. Wright himself, however, preferred his sister Jane's birth year of 1869 and took that year as his own. Wright's autobiography confuses dates further: he wrote that in 1866 his mother Anna was 29 years old and his father 17 years older. In fact Anna Lloyd Jones was born in Wales in 1839 and arrived in America in 1845. At the time of her marriage to William Cary Wright in 1866 she was 27 years old—although she led everyone to believe that she was 24. William Russell Cary Wright—there was no "Russell" in his name and this appears to be another Wrightian invention—came from Hartford, Connecticut according to Frank. In fact, Wright Senior was born in Westfield, Massachusetts in 1825 at a time when his father (Frank's grandfather) the Reverend David Wright was serving

ABOVE: The young Frank Lloyd Wright.

PREVIOUS PAGE: The Stockman House, Mason City, Iowa was built in 1908.

in the area as a Baptist minister. Wright's penchant for and skill in altering facts to suit his purposes—he would tell different people different things at different times—makes sorting fact from fiction in his writings a difficult task. It even turns out that the most famous name in American architecture may, after all, not be Wright's real name!

At birth and for some years after it appears that he was called Frank *Lincoln* Wright. His father, who was at various times a lawyer, a preacher, and a music teacher, was known throughout Wisconsin as a fine orator. Following President Lincoln's assassination in 1865, many public eulogies were delivered across America and Wright was

chosen to preside over the ceremonies held on the court house lawn in Richland Center. The following year Wright married Anna (then called Hannah) Lloyd Jones and their first child was born 10 months later. Like many sons born in the years following Lincoln's death, it would not be surprising that the middle name of Lincoln was given to baby Frank.

Two Wright family documents support this thesis and document the name Lincoln. The family oral tradition also continued to favor it over Lloyd, mainly because many of the Wrights felt that Anna had altered her son's name after her relationship with her husband had deteriorated into open warfare. Frank was undoubtedly Anna's favorite child and it seems that she confirmed "ownership" of her son by giving him part of her own name to replace the one that, presumably, her husband had chosen.

Wright's own manipulation of the facts of his name and the date of his birth were just a small part of his continuous efforts to successfully create a sense of mystery and a mythology around himself. Other "mysteries" in the Wright family saga include how Anna, in the middle years of the 19th century and growing up in near isolation on a farm in the Midwest, decided on architecture as the profession for her sure-to-be-genius son. At this time architecture was not the profession it is today. Lacking the prestige of medicine or law, architects were more often than not building contractors or even carpenters. The first school of architecture in the United States—at Massachusetts Institute of Technology—did not open its doors until a year after Frank's birth and then boasted a grand total of four students. The one big city within easy reach of Spring Green was

Chicago, but it was not until after the great fire in 1871 that the city became a magnet for architects.

According to Wright's "mythology," his mother was inspired by the wood engravings of English cathedrals which decorated Frank's nursery. This account, however, raises several problems: the first is that Anna was a Unitarian, a religion that shunned ecclesiastical embellishment. To the Unitarians, the Gothic cathedrals of England with their origins in Catholicism were at odds with their own simple beliefs and plain wooden meeting houses. Second, it appears that the wood engravings themselves, which Wright as a babe in his cradle supposedly gazed on, were in fact published in *Harper's Weekly* between 1878 and 1881—11 years after Wright's birth. Third, Wright spoke of a nursery: he was born in a very small house where already resident were his parents, and three children from his father's first marriage to Permelia Holcomb. It is unlikely that such a room and such decorations ever existed—except in the minds of Anna and her devoted son.

Throughout his autobiography (there are two versions of it: a first edition from 1932 and a second, revised version from 1943) Wright praises his mother. We are told that she was tall and handsome, self-possessed, and with a fiery temper. His father William is depicted in a less flattering light; it is clear that Frank took his mother's side in family arguments and his relationship with her would affect his accounts and recollections of events.

His father, William Wright, was a Baptist and a 41-year old widower with three small children when he married Anna. William had dropped out of college—probably for financial reasons—and had several times given up training in medicine. Eventually he graduated from Madison College (now Colgate University) in 1849. In 1850 he was teaching music in Utica, New York and the following year married one of

ABOVE: Frank Lloyd Wright (seated right) with moustache. Wright's first wife Catherine holds their first-born son Lloyd; his mother Anna sits behind, and between husband and wife; Wright's sister Jane holds a tennis racket; Maginel has her arms over her big brother.

his pupils, Permelia Holcomb. The newlyweds then moved to Hartford where William was an admired preacher and where in 1859 he was admitted to the bar after studying law. By this time Permelia had given birth to two children: the first child died in infancy, the second, Charles William, was born in Hartford in 1856. A third child, George Irving, was born in Providence, Rhode Island in 1858 and the fourth, Elizabeth Amelia, in Belle Plaine, Iowa in 1860. The birthplaces of William's children have often been taken as early evidence of William Wright's itinerant behavior, yet it was not uncommon for families to relocate to different states as employment became available. Nevertheless, William Wright's "jack of all trades" existence provided several nails for his coffin which were later to be hammered home by Anna and the Lloyd Jones clan.

Around 1861 Wright and his family were on the move again—this time settling in Lone Rock, Wisconsin, where, although Wright made a good impression and was well liked by the community, he had trouble

supporting his family financially. In order to help out, Permelia took in boarders, one of whom was none other than schoolteacher Anna Lloyd Jones.

Many say that, when Permelia died in childbirth in 1864, Anna set her sights on William Wright. She was 25 years old—in danger of becoming an old maid—but Wright also offered her an existence far removed from her former life on a farm. Wright was educated, a trained lawyer, a composer of music and songs, and played several instruments—some of which he made with his own hands. In less than two years Anna did become his wife, but they were an ill-matched couple from the start. The situation was not helped by the fact that Anna's "tremendous temper," as the Lloyd Jones called it, in fact masked a deeper, more serious mental illness.

ABOVE: Frank Lloyd Wright aged around 35.

After the birth of Frank the family situation worsened: Anna was treating her step-children extremely harshly, often inflicting physical punishment for the slightest of reasons and, fearing for her grandchildren's safety, Permelia's mother arranged for them to live with Holcomb relatives. This meant that the children by his first wife were to grow up far removed from the father who loved them dearly. For Anna, the step-children no longer existed and even Frank in adult life made no effort to contact his father (or even attend his funeral) and little effort to contact his half-brothers and half-sister.

In 1869 Frank's sister Jane was born and nine years later Margaret Ellen, known as Maginel. William Wright and his daughters were left in no doubt that Frank was the apple of his mother's eye and Frank himself appears to have accepted the situation with a good deal of satisfaction, believing that the situation was quite "natural" since both were convinced of his genius!

The relationship between Anna and William was steadily deteriorating: Anna was treating her husband with open contempt and soon she would proclaim her hatred and refuse to have sexual relations with him.

Despite family difficulties, William Wright moved his family east in order to take up the position of minister at a Baptist church in Weymouth, a prosperous suburb of Boston, Massachusetts. Boston was undoubtedly the intellectual center of the country and, although the family was not well-off, Anna was able to buy the latest books and to attend concerts and lectures. In 1876 the family made a holiday journey to Philadelphia to visit the Centennial Exposition being held there. Although it is uncertain whether Frank visited the fair—he makes mention neither of doing so nor of the two Japanese buildings that had been erected there—it is known that Anna visited the fair, because it was here that she encountered for the first time the educational toys called "Gifts," which took the form of colored strips of paper, two-dimensional geometric grids, wooden spheres, blocks, and pyramids. These were designed so that mothers and school teachers could train children following the educational philosophy of Friedrich Froebel, the German inventor of the kindergarten.

Froebel had developed a series of exercises designed to educate a child's sensory experience of the world through play. Though Frank at age nine and his sister Jane at seven were well beyond kindergarten age, they both, like their mother, became enamored with Froebel's system. In later years, Frank Lloyd Wright regularly cited the Froebel "Gifts" as one of the most profound influences on his approach to architecture. Indeed, many of Wright's buildings have been said to be derived from basic Froebelian forms. Wright himself noted that his habit of designing on a modular plan directly paralleled the exercises in which Froebel encouraged children to arrange

wooden blocks on a two-dimensional grid to create geometric patterns and structures. The Froebel method gave Wright the basis for his fascination with a small number of geometric shapes, which in different combinations were used throughout his architectural career: the spiral, the sphere, and the circle, the square, and the cube, the triangle, and the tetrahedron.

Froebel's kindergarten exercises went beyond merely breaking up complex shapes into their constituent parts and assembling them in a different order. Froebel intended that the children should associate the different shapes with symbolic meanings. This was an approach for which Wright was to argue when he stated that certain geometric forms symbolized human ideas, moods, and sentiments. For Wright, the circle symbolized infinity; the triangle, structural unity; the

ABOVE: Wright in the drafting room at his summer headquarters, Taliesin, at Spring Green, Wisconsin.

LEFT: A view of the octagonal drafting room of Wright's Studio at Oak Park.

spire, aspiration; the spiral, organic progress; and the square, integrity.

Froebel's educational system also helps to throw light on Wright's later relationship to nature. Froebel believed that his pupils should not make drawings or any other representations direct from objects until they had spent many months working on his geometric exercises. In this way Froebel believed that children would understand the geometries that organized and structured the outward appearance of the world and its objects. This explains why Wright, who constantly referred to his work as "organic" or "natural," could also avoid including naturalistic designs in his structures. Instead, Wright preferred for his deco-

rative motifs highly abstract, geometrical patterns, which do not look like the natural forms they represent, but are the essence of those forms. The best-known examples are the stained glass, the cast concrete, and the copper plant motifs associated with certain Wright buildings: the tulips at the Oak Park House and Studio (1889–98); the sumac at the Susan Lawrence Dana House in Springfield (1902); the hollyhock at the Aline Barnsdall "Hollyhock House" in Los Angeles (1916–21) and the "Tree of Life" at the Darwin D. Martin House in Buffalo (1904).

In addition to the Froebel "Gifts" which she bestowed on her son, a further contribution to Wright's development—in this instance his "spiritual" development—came from Anna and the Lloyd Jones relatives. From them Wright acquired his sense of family identity as well as his religious and philosophical outlook. The Lloyd Jones had a tradition of religious dissent which mixed

together Unitarianism and Welsh non-conformist beliefs with the intellectualism of the New England Transcendentalists—Emerson, Thoreau, and Whitman—into a form of liberal Protestantism that was suspicious of any orthodox religion that interfered with the individual's quest for spiritual truth. The Lloyd Jones's belief was summed up in the family motto: "Truth Against the World." Unity was their watchword and when the family built its own small church in 1886, and gave a 19-year old Frank his first experience in architecture, it was called Unity Chapel.

Wright's own commitment to Unitarianism, and to the principles of spiritual unity it promoted, continued throughout his life and one of his first large public buildings turned out to be Unity Temple, built in 1905–08 for the Unitarian congregation of Oak Park, Illinois. In the 1930s Wright formally joined the First Unitarian Society in Madison, Wisconsin and 10 years later designed its famous meeting house. When he set up the Taliesin Fellowship, Wright included Sunday morning gatherings at which, in a form of Unitarian service, the assembled community listened to classical music, readings from favorite writers, and lectures from Wright on architecture, morality, and life.

In 1878 William Wright and his growing family were on the move again, quitting Weymouth for Madison and a house on the shores of Lake Mendota. Thanks to the new trains running between Madison and Spring Green, the Lloyd Jones's family farm at Hillside was now accessible and was to be where Frank would spend his summers. Nevertheless, this future devotee and advocate of nature found these summer stays a grueling and physically exhausting experience: unlike the athletic physiques of the Lloyd Jones's family, Frank had inherited the Wrights' small-framed body, and although in maturity Wright claimed to be 5ft 8½in tall, without the built-up heels on his shoes he was closer to 5ft 6in.

In 1884, with their relationship having broken down beyond repair, William Wright brought divorce proceedings against Anna on the grounds that she had "wilfully deserted" him. Acting on the advice of her family, Anna did not contest the divorce and received custody of the children and possession of the house.

School at this time appeared difficult for Frank: although he was intelligent and a voracious reader, he consistently earned low grades and repeatedly dropped out of school. Failing to graduate from high school, he nevertheless entered the University of Wisconsin as a special student. During his brief stay he held a job as a student-assistant to Allen D. Conover, Professor of Engineering at the university. Conover had recently opened an architectural practice in Madison and hired Wright as a favor to Anna. For carrying out a variety of more or less menial tasks Wright was paid $35 a month. Importantly, Conover also introduced Wright to the rudiments of civil engineering and draftsmanship, and the whole experience seems to have encouraged Wright to drop out of university and opt for education in "the real world."

Wright decided to go to Chicago. The decision, however, did not meet with support from Anna, who sought advice from her brother Jenkin Lloyd Jones, one of the leading preachers in the city and at the time in the process of building a new church there. Jenkin agreed that Chicago was no place for the young Frank, a view that encouraged Wright even more to leave immediately for the city. Pawning some books that his father had left behind after the divorce, Wright got together enough money for a railroad ticket, leaving him with $7—enough for food and lodging until he found a job.

In 1887 Chicago was a booming city where Wright saw his first electric light bulb, his first cable car, and his first ballet performance at the Chicago Opera House. According to his autobiography he spent four days trudging the streets seeking work at various architectural practices. On the fourth day he went to the office of Joseph L. Silsbee, coincidentally the architect of his uncle Jenkin Lloyd Jones's new church. But Wright had resolved not to use his family connection with Silsbee: it was on the strength of drawings he had taken along to the meeting and on the recommendation of one of Silsbee's draftsmen, Cecil Corwin, that he was hired immediately.

Much as he enjoyed working with Silsbee, whose influence—particularly in his use of a Queen Anne style of architecture, which Wright would also use in his early career, and his taste for oriental pictorial art in the form of Japanese prints—would remain indelibly marked on Wright, after a few months he felt that he had learned all he could. Furthermore, like all beginners, he felt that he was sorely underpaid. Having secured a position with the architect W.W. Clay, Wright soon changed his mind: he was rapidly out of his depth and returned to Silsbee. The return of the prodigal was short-lived since Wright, ever restless—perhaps a trait inherited from his father—applied for an opening in the drafting rooms at Adler and Sullivan, the firm then at work in preparing drawings for the Auditorium Building, which would make the firm famous from coast to coast. When Wright arrived at the firm in 1887, it was Louis Sullivan who hired him because he needed a draftsman with a talent for drawing in a manner that would be close to his own. By the time the Auditorium Building was built in 1890, Wright had been appointed head draftsman and was privileged with his own office next door to Sullivan—he called him his *Lieber Meister* (German for "dear master")—situated at the top of the romantic tower of the Auditorium Building itself.

Anna had refused to be left behind when Wright went to work for Silsbee, and she and her daughters promptly moved to Oak Park. Unlike most young men wanting to make their way in the world, therefore, Wright continued to live at home but, as with most breadwinners, he took part in the usual round of social activities in the neighborhood. The only way he would escape his mother's apron strings was to marry. During the course of a social gathering at Uncle Jenkin's church, Wright met Catherine Tobin. Despite objections to the courtship by his mother, Wright and Catherine were married after he had secured from Sullivan a five-year contract of employment and a $5,000 loan to buy a plot of land and to build a house.

By all accounts, the wedding ceremony was a disaster: the funereal atmosphere was enhanced by rainy weather. Wright's mother fainted, Catherine's father was in tears as was Uncle Jenkin, who performed the ceremony. To finish off, the newlyweds spent their honeymoon surrounded by the Lloyd Jones at Hillside.

From the moment that Wright and his wife moved into their Oak Park home, he started to alter it. First the plain glass windows were replaced with diamond panes of leaded glass. Following the birth of their first child, Frank Lloyd Wright Junior later shortened to Lloyd, and over the next 13 years five more children—John, Catherine, David, Frances, and Llewellyn—Wright expanded the house and the adjoining studio as a sort of living laboratory of architectural experiments in space and materials. In order to pick up extra money—Wright consistently failed to accumulate savings, habitually lived beyond his means, and was well known as being slow to pay bills—he began designing residential commissions which he called his "bootlegged houses." Adler and Sullivan were largely engaged on large projects and were too busy to undertake domestic commissions. When friends came to ask for designs, they were often turned over to Wright. Wright simply extended the practice by taking on commissions without his employers' knowledge.

A number of reasons have been suggested for the departure of Wright on less than amicable terms from Adler and Sullivan: Wright's growing reputation independent of the firm has often been cited, but there was also a suggestion that Wright had been asked by Sullivan to buy Oriental rugs on his behalf and that Wright had kept a proportion of the money. Whatever the reason—and Wright himself sheds no further light on the subject except to say that he felt challenged by the new opportunities facing him—Wright and Sullivan parted company.

Immediately after quitting the firm, Wright and his friend Cecil Corwen rented space in the tower of the Schiller building on Randolph Street in Chicago—ironically a building that had been designed by Adler and Sullivan a few years earlier and one to which Wright himself contributed. The partnership with Corwen was also to end, however, when Corwen moved back east. Laggard in paying the rent, Wright was forced to move from the Schiller building to Steinway Hall and share loft space there with a number of young architects, among them Robert Spencer, Dwight Perkins, and Myron Hunt. Most of Wright's designing took place at the Oak Park studio where he accumulated a number of young assistants. As Wright's reputation grew, his work would take him further away than Chicago and its suburb of Oak Park; yet he was constantly beset by debt. When Ward Willits invited the Wrights to accompany his wife and himself on a trip to Japan in 1905, Wright borrowed $5,000 from Walter Burley Griffin to help make the trip possible: it is likely that most of the money went on paying existing debts to local traders. Later, Wright and Griffin were to argue over the loan, which Wright refused to pay off. The debt was finally settled when Wright handed over to Griffin a large number of Japanese prints that he had accumulated.

In 1909 Wright's life abruptly changed. In the autumn of that year, he abandoned his wife and six children in Oak Park and left for

Europe with Martha Borthwick Cheney. Mrs. Cheney was always affectionately known as "Mamah." (This was pronounced "May-mah"; Cheney was pronounced "Chee-ny.") Wright's affair with Mrs. Cheney, the wife of his client Edwin Cheney for whom Wright at the time was designing a house, had been going on for some time, but there were probably other reasons why Wright wanted to leave: he had for several years been corresponding with C.R. Ashbee, who had always urged Wright to visit the Guild of Handicrafts in the Gloucestershire town of Chipping Campden, England. Wright had also received a letter from German publisher Ernst Wasmuth, offering to publish a complete monograph of his work. Wright asked Catherine for a divorce, but his wife asked that they remain married

for a year, at the end of which if he still wanted a divorce, she would give him one.

Wright and Mamah Cheney spent a year abroad, with the first months devoted largely to the production of the Wasmuth folio. For lovers, their living arrangements were odd to say the least: Mrs. Cheney rented an apartment in Berlin, while Wright rented an apartment in Florence. The remainder of their stay was in Fiesole, Italy, where Wright said they were engaged in translating excerpts from Goethe. The translations were no doubt Mamah Cheney's work since Wright knew little German beyond the words "Lieber Meister."

Wright's flight from Oak Park was a well-publicized scandal. Even more shocking was his return to Oak Park. During his year abroad Wright still had his usual expenses—the support of his family and remaining debts—but now he was faced with the bur-

ABOVE: Wright displaying a model of a prefabricated house in 1958—a year before his death after 72 years of work. During the whole of that time his answer to the question "What is your favorite project?" was "The next one!"

den of the rents on the Berlin and Florence apartments, the Fiesole villa, sightseeing costs, and the costs of printing the Wasmuth folio—Wright had bought the entire edition and would have to wait many years to recoup his investment. But on his return commissions were few: few clients were prepared to be associated with a philanderer and an unrepentant one at that, since Mrs. Cheney continued to be Wright's mistress.

In spite of mounting debts, on his return to the United States Wright threw his energies into Taliesin, a home designed on a lavish scale. The stream in the valley below the house at Hillside was partly dammed to create both a pleasure lake and, by means of a hydraulic ram, a supply of water for the stone reservoir at the top of the hill. From there the water fell by gravity to the house, to its pools, and fountains, barns, and other farm buildings, and onto the vegetable gardens on the lower slopes of the hill. This was

to be his "kingdom," with the hope that it would be a recreation ground for his children, grandchildren, and great-grandchildren.

By the autumn of 1911 Taliesin was sufficiently complete for Mamah Borthwick (she returned to her maiden name following her divorce in the summer of the same year) to move in with Wright. Dividing his time between Taliesin and a Chicago office, commissions began to return to Wright and by 1913 he had received two of the most important commissions of his career: the Imperial Hotel in Tokyo and the Midway Gardens complex in Chicago.

All looked to be going well for Wright until the summer of 1914 when disaster struck. While at work in Chicago on the Midway Gardens project, he received the news that Taliesin had been destroyed by

fire. Killed in the fire, that had been set by crazed cook Julian Carleton, were Mrs. Cheney and her two children; draftsman Emil Brodelle; Ernest Weston, the young son of William Weston (one of Wright's favorite carpenters at Taliesin), and two handymen—David Lindblom and Thomas Brunker. Carleton was found alive, but had attempted suicide by swallowing hydrochloric acid. Arrested he was taken to Dodgeville jail where he died of starvation—because his throat was so badly burned by the acid—seven weeks later giving no explanation for his arson attack.

Despite Wright's grief, Taliesin II was to grow out of the charred ruins of Taliesin I and, grieving the loss of one mistress, Wright took a second, Miriam Noel. The relationship was not a happy one: in public Wright praised Mrs. Noel while in private they argued constantly. Some of Miriam's letters to Wright were intercepted by a housekeeper, Nellie Breen (whom Wright had dismissed).

Breen passed the letters to the newspapers for publication and then instituted an action in the Federal courts asking that Wright be indicted for violating the Mann Act—a statute passed in Congress in 1910 which prohibited the transportation of women across state lines for "immoral purposes." Wright's defense counsel was none other than Clarence Darrow—the lawyer who successfully defended in the Dayton "monkey" trial of 1925 John T. Scopes, the schoolteacher who taught the theory of evolution. Darrow succeeded in getting the case dismissed. Despite a six-year long strained relationship, when Wright was finally divorced from Catherine in 1922, he and Miriam were married as soon as the law allowed. The wedding took place in the middle of a bridge crossing the Wisconsin River, just upstream from Taliesin.

Wright's second marriage was to be as turbulent as his first, and within a year of the wedding to Miriam, Wright had a new mistress—Olga Ivanovna Milonov Hinzenberg. Known as Olgivanna, she had been born in Cetinje in Montenegro, educated in Russia and Turkey, and in her teens had married Russian architect Vladimir Hinzenberg. The couple had a daughter, Svetlana. Hinzenberg was a naturalized American citizen who lived in Chicago. He and Olgivanna had been separated for some years—she lived in France at the Gurdjieff Institute for the Harmonious Development of Man. Olgivanna had been giving a dance exhibition in New York before traveling to Chicago to settle some family matters when she and Wright met during a ballet performance. Throughout the autumn of 1924 Wright ardently pursued Olgivanna and by early in the new year they were lovers.

Olgivanna obtained a divorce and Wright hoped to divorce Miriam. Matters became more urgent when Olgivanna discovered she was pregnant and, in December 1925, she gave birth to daughter Iovanna.

ABOVE: Frank Lloyd Wright worked on well past the age that most people retire, helped by his ardent followers.

Miriam vacillated over the terms of the divorce and gave interviews to the press which once again put Wright—the man—in the spotlight. No doubt Miriam felt that she had been ousted not only from her marriage but also from Taliesin, her rightful home, where Olgivanna and her daughters now lived. Miriam filed a suit against Olgivanna for alienation of affection while Olgivanna's ex-husband secured injunctions against the removal of Svetlana out of America. Once again Wright found himself charged under the Mann Act: shortly after Iovanna's birth, Wright had taken Olgivanna on a holiday to Puerto Rico which, unknown to him, amounted to a technical violation of Olgivanna's status as an illegal alien in the United States. During a family break at Lake Minnetonka in Minnesota, Wright was arrested and spent the night in jail.

Wright and family spent the winter of 1927 in La Jolla, California. In February, a fire at Taliesin did several thousand dollars worth of damage to the building, to his books, and to drawings. At the insistence of his creditors, Wright's large and valuable collection of Japanese prints—one of the finest in the country, valued at over $100,000—was sold at auction for less than $40,000, leaving him a total of $43,000 in debt. Fortunately, the Wisconsin Savings Bank offered him a year's grace in order to pay off his debts and regain possession of Taliesin. Meanwhile Miriam at last agreed to a divorce.

A year went by and Wright could not raise the money to retake Taliesin from the Bank of Wisconsin. Fortunately, however, friends came to his aid. (Throughout his career Wright would always be lucky enough to find friends and clients to support him, his charisma outweighing his inability to stick to deadlines and estimated costs.) This group of friends—including Darwin D. Martin, Mrs. Avery Coonley, designer Joseph Urban, Wright's sisters Jane and Maginel, and writer

Alexander Woollcott—established a corporation, Frank Lloyd Wright Incorporated, the purpose of which was to free Wright of debt but which would also technically own the income from his work. The corporation would give Wright an allowance sufficient to live on but not large enough to buy thousands of dollars worth of extravagant luxuries—particularly automobiles for which he had a passion—in a single spree which was his habit. Wright, Inc. managed to arrange a deal with the bank and gained possession of Taliesin in the name of the corporation.

Wright's marriage to Olgivanna in 1928 provided him with a stability that allowed him to focus his energies in spite of the few commissions during the years of the great depression of the 1930s. With Olgivanna's encouragement, Wright assembled a fellowship that would support his work and his beliefs for the rest of his career and continues today, beyond his death. The Taliesin Fellowship, as it became known, served as Wright's office, a school, and a communal family that Wright believed was essential for the growth and development of his ideas, since it allowed him to extend the concept of organic architecture into a lifestyle in which apprentices labored in the fields, undertook household chores, and drafted and construct-

ed buildings to create a unified approach to understanding architecture.

Public awareness of Wright and his ideas was furthered by lecture tours and the publication of *An Autobiography* in 1932. Though commissions were few, Wright was nevertheless busy: there was the Broadacre City project for a four square mile settlement for 1,400 families; the project for a house on the Mesa (1931), and a trip to Russia. The decade culminated with the completion of Wright's most recognized buildings since the Imperial Hotel in Tokyo: the S.C. Johnson and Son Incorporated Administration Building in Racine, Wisconsin (1936–39); "Fallingwater," the house for Edgar J. Kaufmann in Mill Run, Pennsylvania (1934–37) and the Usonian "Honeycomb House" for Paul R. and Jean S. Hanna in Palo Alto, California (1935–37).

Yet it was the 1940s that were to be some of the most productive years of Wright's career and the decade in which Wright's architecture became both nationally and internationally recognized. At this time Wright was increasingly interested in function and technology, including the accumulation of light for solar heating and earthbern insulation. Wright's interpretations of materials and technologies in his own

"metaphorical" way was key to the development of the "Usonian" houses which flourished in the 1940s.

Unlike many other architects who believed that modern housing could be built in factories and shipped to site, Wright believed that, while the future of domestic architecture was in mass production of building components like sheet metal screens, the finished houses should not themselves become standardized: each was to be individual and suit the needs of the inhabitants.

In 1946 Wright unveiled his plans for the Solomon R. Guggenheim Museum. In the 16 years it took to build, the museum underwent several design changes. Contributing further to the delay were New York building regulations that specified an emergency exit on each floor. The problem in the museum was that there was only one floor, but it spiraled around and up! The Guggenheim was the culmination of Wright's pursuit of space as the inner reality of architecture. It embodies all Wright's lifelong interests in architectural archetypes, which many see as having their origins in Froebel's Gifts: the museum is a three-dimensional spiral turned on its head to create the outwardly expanding interior exhibition space.

By the last decade of his life, organic architecture for Wright was still the "true" modern architecture. Writing in *The Future of Architecture* (1953) at the age of 86, Wright devised nine key words to clarify his meaning of organic architecture:

- "Nature," which meant not just living things but was the essence of materials, plans and feelings.
- "Organic" referred to the relationship of parts to the whole.
- "Form and function" were one, unified.

RIGHT: Wright photographed while working on the Solomon R. Guggenheim Museum—his finest non-domestic project and a remarkable tribute to an innovative designer.

- "Romance" was the creative force expressed by each individual embodied in the form of architecture.
- "Tradition" did not mean imitating the past, but implied a sense of belonging.
- "Ornament" was the emotional expression that was integral to, and to be integrated into, architecture, and which revealed and enhanced the structure of the building.
- "Spirit" was the essential life force within an object.
- The "Third Dimension" was the intrinsic depth of a building.
- "Space" was the "invisible fountain, from which all rhythm flows to which they must pass."

To these nine defining terms, Wright added a tenth: "Democracy"—the national ideal which Wright defined as the gospel of individuality. Mixing these ideas, originally expressed some 50 years earlier, with experiments in technology and building materials, allowed Wright to realize his ambition to build a skyscraper—the Price Company Tower in Bartlesville, Oklahoma, which was designed and constructed from 1952 to 1956.

In his last few years Wright had several commissions for religious buildings. The one which for most commentators demonstrates his ideas of an integrated structure, materials, building technology, and purpose is the Beth Sholom Synagogue in Elkins Park, Pennsylvania (1953–59). In its imagery Wright intended the building to symbolize the rock from which Moses descended with the Ten Commandments. Entering the synagogue, worshippers could feel as though they had entered a light-filled crystal at whose metaphorical center was the holy word of God.

On April 4, 1959, aged 91, a few days after celebrating Easter at Taliesin West with members of his family and Fellowship, Wright was taken to hospital in Phoenix, Arizona complaining of stomach pains. He was operated on for an intestinal obstruction and astounded his doctors by surviving the operation. He appeared to be making a good recovery but, in the late evening of April 9, the nurse on duty heard him give a sigh and Frank Lloyd Wright died.

Following a precedent established by Wright in the burial of his beloved Mamah Borthwick Cheney about half a century earlier, his body was taken from Phoenix to Taliesin North. His coffin was placed on a horse-drawn farm wagon and transported to the family burial ground, at the foot of the hill a few hundred yards from Taliesin, where it was interred close to the graves of Mamah Cheney and the other decisive woman in his life, his mother.

This was not to be Wright's final resting place, however. When Olgivanna died in 1985, her last wishes were that her husband's body be brought to Taliesin West in Arizona. There his ashes were mingled with Olgivanna's and buried in a new grave.

IN CONTEXT

Frank Lloyd Wright's architecture occurred in six phases. His earliest work was to some extent a derivation of the work of the leading architects of the 1880s including H.H. Richardson, Bruce Price, and McKim, Mead & White, whose work was widely publicized in contemporary magazines. The second phase—in the 1890s—is classical in nature. Furthermore, the decoration Wright used in these years is evidence of the influence of Louis Sullivan, for whom Wright worked for five years.

The third phase, sometimes called Wright's "First Golden Age," began in 1901 and extended into the 1910s. In this phase Wright created a distinctly American house type—the Prairie House—characterized by a strong horizontality, a use of natural materials, and a close attention to the links between the building and its site.

From the 1910s, the decorative use of Mayan-inspired cast concrete dominated and culminated in Wright's fourth phase, the textile-block houses in the Los Angeles area of California. Wright's fifth and most productive period featured the Usonian House, a lower-cost house type than the Prairie House. Finally there are buildings from throughout Wright's career, the large scale, non-domestic commissions, which are distinguished either by their innovative design or by the quality of their engineering. Some, such as the Larkin Building (1903), Midway Gardens (1914), and the Imperial Hotel, Tokyo (1915) no longer exist, while others—Unity Church (1904), the S.C. Johnson Wax company headquarters (1936), the Solomon R. Guggenheim Museum (1956), and the Marin County Civic Center (1957)—are not only landmarks in modern American architecture but are also publicly accessible.

ABOVE: John Ruskin (1819-1900), author of *The Seven Lamps of Architecture* (1849) and *The Stones of Venice* (1851), established the criteria for judging art and architecture that were followed in the 19th and early 20th centuries.

PREVIOUS PAGE: Taliesin North—as the Spring Green "colony" was called—was to be Wright's summer headquarters: winters were spent at Taliesin West in Arizona.

Each phase of Wright's architecture was marked by identifying themes—organicism, the prairies of the Midwest of America, and the search for an American identity through architecture. Yet in all of his phases Wright related the meaning of his architecture to the order of nature. Wright believed that by correlating a building to nature, the spiritual condition of mankind could be elevated. In arguing for an "organic architec-ture" that emulated the principles of nature without imitating its forms, Wright joined the ranks of some of the most influential thinkers of the 19th century.

Organic Architecture

Wright's concept of organic architecture evolved from a set of principles in the 1890s. In 1894 he wrote an essay "In the Cause of Architecture" (not published until 1908) in which he formulated six design principles that defined organic architecture. The first was that the measures of art were simplicity and repose. In order to achieve these qualities, everything that was unnecessary—including interior dividing walls—had to be eliminated. For Wright, buildings had as few rooms as possible and openings from one to the other were part of the structure and form of the buildings, while details like decoration, fixtures, and furniture were to be integrated into the overall structure.

Wright's second principle called for as many different styles of houses as there were "styles" of people. In this way Wright believed that his designs could provide each of his clients with a house that expressed their individuality. A multiplicity of styles also meant that architects no longer had to rely on the historical styles that had dominated 19th century architecture, and which in America often had no relation to that country's own history.

Wright's third principle linked together nature, the landscape, or the building site and the architecture. He wrote that buildings should appear to "grow" from the site and should be shaped to harmonize with their surroundings. Likewise, in his fourth principle, Wright stated that the colors of buildings should be derived from nature and should be adapted to harmonize with the building materials. In his essay Wright used the term "conventionalization." By this he meant the abstraction of plant colors and forms as the source of his design motifs.

Wright's fifth principle of organic architecture concerned the expression of the "nature of materials." The materials used in buildings—whether wood, brick, stone, or plaster—should look like wood, brick, stone, or plaster. Each material should show its natural texture, grain, and color and not be "disguised" to look like another material. Wright believed that "natural" materials were "friendly" and beautiful, but also that the nature of the materials was inextricably linked to the idea of the structure of the building. In this way, the structural system of load and support would be apparent through the use of the materials.

The sixth of Wright's principles expressed his belief that buildings should have qualities that were analogous to the human qualities of truth, sincerity, and beauty and that buildings should bring people joy.

To a large extent, Wright's principles were similar to the ideas that were current in the Arts and Crafts movement. In a sense, the Arts and Crafts movement was not a true movement, but more a widespread group of individuals and individualistic designers who had a kindred spirit—an allegiance to creating an organic art and architecture that owed its origins to A.W.N. Pugin (1812–52), John Ruskin (1819–1900), and William Morris (1834–96).

The Arts and Crafts Movement

A critic of contemporary 19th century industrial life, Pugin sought a simpler and more functional design aesthetic that he believed had once existed in a pre-industrial England. Rejecting the classical styles—derived from Greece and Rome—Pugin instead advocated the naturalism and asymmetricality of Gothic ornamentation. Although not a pioneer of the Gothic revival, Pugin was nevertheless

the first to link the style with a moral dimension: he believed that the Gothic style expressed the morals and values of order, stability, a sense of community, and a joy in labor (which to Pugin had been exposed in the medieval period's greatest artistic achievement—the great Gothic cathedrals) that were lacking in 19th century life.

In 1836 Pugin published his *Contrasts*, in which he compared the medieval and the Victorian periods and found the latter wanting. In the 19th century, Pugin saw the lack of standards in design as an expression of the deterioration in the quality of life. Only by returning to Gothic principles did Pugin believe that standards could be restored. In *Contrasts* Pugin set down two rules for design: the first was that there should be no features about a building which were not necessary for "convenience, construction or propriety," and second, that all ornament should be part of the essential structure of the building. Pugin's aim to reunite art and labor, designers and craftsmen, and the spiritual with everyday life was to provide the foundations for the Arts and Crafts Movement, but, unlike his followers Ruskin and Morris, Pugin advocated the use of machinery in the production of art and design. In his *Apology for the Present Revival of Christian Architecture in England* published in 1843, Pugin stated that his intention was not to "turn back the clock" and that he was not opposed to technology and machinery *per se*, but that he wanted machinery to be confined to "legitimate" uses, such as the relief of boredom for workers engaged in mundane, repetitive tasks.

In contrast, Ruskin declared that all cast and machine-produced work was "bad" and was not "honest labor." For Ruskin, factories had interfered with the natural rhythms of life and those who had been creative individual craftsmen were now anonymous laborers. Like the products they were now making, these laborers had lost their uniqueness. Only by returning to handcrafting,

ABOVE: William Morris (1834–1896) defined art as "the expression by man of his pleasure in labor." But while Morris abhorred the machine, Wright was to advocate machine production as the natural extension of the principles of the Arts and Crafts Movement.

BELOW: Walt Whitman (1819–1892) was one of the handful of people whom Wright acknowledged as an "influence" in his 1957 A Testament.

could individuality and quality in design be restored.

Ruskin's two most famous books, *The Seven Lamps of Architecture* (1849) and *The Stones of Venice* (1851), established criteria for judging art and architecture that were to be followed well into the 20th century. In the former, Ruskin declared that true architecture was distinguished from mere buildings by the application of ornament. Ornament was "legitimate" only if it followed his strict rules of "honesty": ornament must be derived from nature and must be true to the materials in which it was made.

While Ruskin was one of the most widely read English authors, more far reaching in his influence was William Morris, who to most people is the embodiment of Arts and Crafts principles, blending arts, ideals, and business. Emulating Morris's example were a number of organizations such as the Century Guild, founded in 1882 by A.H. Mackmurdo and Selwyn Image. Two years later Mackmurdo launched *The Hobby Horse*, a magazine that was the vehicle for the most advanced artistic and literary thought of the period. *The Hobby Horse* would not only be an inspiration for the Boston-based periodical *Knight Errant* in 1892, but was the forerunner of *The Studio* magazine (1893), the journal most responsible for spreading the Arts and Crafts Movement abroad.

The Art Workers Guild, which was founded in London in 1884, grew into the Arts and Crafts Exhibition Society, and to great public acclaim it displayed more than 500 objects at the New Gallery in 1888. By 1897 the first organizations modeled after the Exhibition Society were established in America, and the Boston Society of Arts and Crafts was soon followed by organizations in Chicago, New York, Minneapolis, and Detroit. Within 10 years across America, through the medium of exhibitions, journals, and salesrooms, hundreds of societies were engaged in the manufacture of Arts and Crafts products.

One of the most significant figures in the Anglo-American cultural exchange was C.R. Ashbee (1863–1942). Ashbee knew both Louis Sullivan and Frank Lloyd Wright and in 1911 he would write the introduction to the German publication by Ernst Wasmuth of Wright's work. The themes that Ashbee expressed—politics and reform, contemplation, ornament, and nature—culminated in the Guild of Handicrafts in 1888. Ashbee believed that the most important product of labor was pleasure, and therefore members of his guild did not have to be expert craftsmen because good design and good products would evolve simply from having the right attitude to work. For Ashbee, America offered a new opportunity to develop further the aims and ideals of the Arts and Crafts movement. But as much as the American Arts and Crafts movement owed a debt to European sources, it was itself also the product of many designers' quests for a truly American style.

An American Vision

Ashbee's own journals of his visits to America between 1896 and 1915 document the importance of the group of writers and artists known as the Transcendentalists, which included Ralph Waldo Emerson, Henry David, Thoreau, and Walt Whitman. Despite widespread industrialization, even in the last years of the 19th century, American life was still close to the spirit of the "frontiersman." New areas were "colonized" in their own way free from the burden of historical influence. Unlike Europe, America was largely free from the weight of the past and the influence of nature was keenly felt.

As well as serving as a sort of role model for the "romantic genius"—something that Wright wholeheartedly embraced particularly after 1909 when he abandoned his family and embarked on a scandalous affair with Mamah Cheney—when Wright spoke of "organic architecture" (a way of building that would look to nature for its models and inspiration) Wright was using the word "nature" in a Transcendentalist way. Nature's value, in this sense, was primarily spiritual: natural forms were "dead matter" until they were touched by the human spirit and it was the role of humans—especially artists—to breathe life into the "dead matter" by relating it to the whole of creating and thereby giving it spiritual meaning and value. For Ralph Waldo Emerson, natural beauty was valuable insofar as it reflected divine beauty. For Wright the purpose of art and architecture was not to "copy" the external appearance of nature, but to use it in the way Emerson advised—as an opportunity to explore nature and to express the universal spirit. For Wright nature was the raw material to be transformed into a vision of a divine world.

It is possible that Wright became aware of the writings of Emerson through Louis Sullivan (1856–1924), who was himself a self-confessed admirer of Walt Whitman. In *An Autobiography*, however, Wright makes no mention of Emerson as contributing to his intellectual and artistic development. On the other hand Sullivan, although only 15 years older than Wright, was admiringly called "Lieber Meister," and, along with Walt Whitman (whose disciples referred to him as "*Übermensch*"—superman), was among the very few forerunners whom Wright officially recognized.

Louis Sullivan was born in Boston and during his youth spent many of his summers with his grandparents in South Reading, Massachusetts. It was here that Sullivan's adoration of nature developed. In 1872 Sullivan enrolled on the new architectural program at Massachusetts Institute of Technology but stayed for only one year before going to work for Frank Furness (1839–1912), the architect of a number of High Victorian Gothic buildings in

ABOVE AND BELOW: Two designs from Owen Jones's book *The Grammar of Ornament* (1856). It was drawings from this book that Wright took to his interview with Sullivan in the fall of 1887.

ABOVE: Dankmar Adler (1844–1900) the other partner in the firm which employed Wright in 1887.

Philadelphia, including the Pennsylvania Academy of Fine Arts (1871–76) and the Provident Life and Trust Company building (1876–79). Sullivan's sojourn in Philadelphia also lasted less than one year and soon he went to Chicago where his family had moved. Between 1873 and 1874 Sullivan was employed in the offices of William Le Baron Jenney (1832–1907), the architect who is generally credited with the construction of the first true skyscraper, the Home Insurance Building in Chicago in 1883.

In the summer of 1874 Sullivan set out for France to complete his education at the École des Beaux Arts in Paris but, once again, he remained for only one year. Nevertheless, it was enough time for him to understand the discipline of academic architecture with its emphasis on functional planning, sound construction techniques, and expressive use of ornament. Sullivan was perhaps the first American architect to consciously explore the relationship between culture and architecture, and the theory of structural rationalism that he developed was derived variously from the ideas of Emerson, and those of Charles Darwin, the sculptor Horatio Greenough, and Owen Jones. The essence of Sullivan's philosophy was the belief that in order to have an architecture that was equal to the society that he hoped would develop in the United States, it was necessary to do away with the outmoded rules and architectural traditions that had been developed in earlier eras and in countries outside America. The version of democracy in the United States was, for Sullivan, a unique development in the history of mankind because it offered the opportunity for each individual to realize their full potential. Consequently, in his search for an appropriate architectural style in which to embody the new world, Sullivan turned to the work of Owen Jones in whose book *The Grammar of Ornament* (1856) he found more than 60 percent of the examples to be far removed from the west: Indian, Celtic, Egyptian, Assyrian, and even Chinese examples became the models for Sullivan's delicate foliate ornamentation. But this ornamentation was always subordinate to the functional requirements of each building.

Sullivan's first major work, the Auditorium Building (1887–89) in Chicago, was built for a business syndicate to house a large civic opera house. But in order to increase the income from the site, it was decided to "wrap" the auditorium inside a hotel and office block. Structurally, the building marked a transitional phase in skyscraper design; the bulk of the complex is 10 storys high, while the entrance to the auditorium itself is underneath a 17-story tower. Outside it uses massive masonry load-bearing walls, while inside, a complex of steel and iron supports the interior and the auditorium balconies and vaults, allowing for unobstructed views of the stage. The interior of the auditorium itself is decorated with low-relief plaster panels of intricate, interlacing foliate forms which are studded with electric light bulbs—Wright would praise highly the way the lighting was integral to the design. Nevertheless Sullivan realized the limitations of this Renaissance "palazzo" architectural language for tall structures and in his next major commissions, the Wainwright Building in St. Louis, Missouri (1890–91) and the Prudential (now Guaranty) Building in Buffalo, New York (1894–95), Sullivan saw his principles of form and function fully in practice. Furthermore, each building uses ornamentation in a way that is complementary to, but does not determine, the overall composition of the building.

Sullivan was to be a major influence on Wright, who joined the firm of Adler and Sullivan in 1887. There are many similarities between the works of the two architects: both believed that ornament was a vital part of architecture but each developed their own modes. Wright's concepts of "organic architecture" and of "democracy in architecture" were also in part derived from Sullivan, who was also to be the moving spirit behind a whole movement of Midwest architecture which thrived from 1900 to 1914: the Prairie School. Architecturally, the approach of the Prairie School consisted of strong, simple overall forms coupled with complex details in an architectural analogy of the broad simple forms of the landscape of the Midwest of America with its "features" of grasses and flowers. Throughout the 1890s Frank Lloyd Wright and a number of young architects—notably Walter Burley Griffin (1876–1937), George Washington Maher (1864–1926), and George Grant Elmslie (1871–1952)—actively pursued the architectural possibilities of this new American idiom. Although Sullivan's intellectual and artistic arguments had made a great impression on these younger designers, in his role as self-proclaimed prophet of cultural democracy Sullivan remained largely ignored. In 1893, the World's Columbian

Exposition in Chicago seriously undermined Sullivan's attempts to introduce America to a fresh approach to architectural design.

The World's Columbian Exposition

To mark the 400th anniversary of the discovery of America by Christopher Columbus, an international exhibition was held in Chicago in 1893. Plans for the exposition began to take shape in 1889 under the guidance of consultant architect John Root (1850–91). Following Root's death, his partner in his architectural firm, Daniel Burnham (1846–1912), was appointed chief of construction. Jackson Park had been selected by the organizers as the site for this World's Fair and the New York-based landscape architect Frederick Law Olmstead (1822–1903)—who had been responsible for the layout of New York's Central Park—was commissioned to design the Chicago layout. The design of the temporary exhibition buildings themselves—decided on by a committee of five architectural firms largely based on the east coast of America—were to be in a classical style for the main buildings, which were arranged formally around the central "Court of Honour." The five "committee" architects were each to design a major building, with five other buildings supplied by Chicago firms. With the notable exception of Sullivan and Alder's Transportation Building, all of the buildings conformed to the classical style and to the guidelines laid down by the organizers.

The most striking feature of Sullivan and Alder's building was the great entrance known as the Golden Door, where a ranked series of Romanesque arches was embellished with Sullivan's signature foliate ornament. Sullivan's intention was to demonstrate the sterility and decadence of the classical styles that surrounded his building by putting forward what he believed was a viable alter-

LEFT: Sullivan combined his interest in tall buildings—his Wainwright Building in St. Louis, Missouri, is seen as the first modern skyscraper and the forerunner of numerous buildings in a similar style.

native. However, although the building was highly praised—particularly by foreign architects—in Chicago, Sullivan's "architecture of the people" was to be rejected largely by the people themselves. The economic depression of the 1890s in America coupled with an increased influx of immigrants created what many people saw as a general state of diversity of cultures and thus the "disintegration" of a single American culture. In order to "reunite" an America at the symbolic centenary of its discovery and on the eve of the 20th century, it was believed by many that a return to "shared values"—based on the highest cultural standards—was required. This belief was to impose a taste for classical architecture and formalistic city planning. Consequently, many architects returned to a Greco-Roman tradition, with the result that many public and commercial buildings—including skyscrapers—as well as numerous private residences, were given grand classical facades and columns suggestive of cleanness,

ABOVE: The World's Columbian Exposition of 1893 was an important point in Wright's career. By this stage he was Sullivan's "right-hand man," and they worked together on the great portal for the Transportation Building

RIGHT: The taste for classical architecture—the "American Renaissance"—was typified by such buildings as New York's Public Library.

unity, order, calmness, and grandeur. Leading examples of the "American Renaissance," as the movement was called, were McKim, Mead & White's Boston Public Library (1887–98) and Pennsylvania Station, New York (1902–11), whose huge waiting room was based on the tepidarium of the Baths of Caracalla in Rome but was at least 25 per cent bigger; Carrere and Hastings' New York Public Library (opened 1911) and Henry Bacon's Lincoln Memorial (designed 1912, completed 1922).

Sullivan, for whom the victory of classical architecture signalled the demise of modern architecture, became increasingly disillusioned with a society which refused to

acknowledge that the development of American architecture was in serious danger. Following the depression of 1893, the cutback on public and private spending meant fewer architectural commissions for the firm and Sullivan's partner, Dankmar Adler, was forced to quit the practice in order to find work to support his family. The years after the Chicago World's Fair were also the years of Sullivan's decline. In the few buildings that he did design—notably small bank buildings in Midwestern cities—Sullivan became increasingly dependent on people who had once been his apprentices. George Grant Elmslie assisted Sullivan until 1909 and was responsible for much of the details, but in conception Sullivan's work increasingly betrayed a debt to his most famous student, Frank Lloyd Wright.

While Wright shared Sullivan's view that the "White City," as the classical core of the World's Fair was dubbed, represented a setback for the new forms of architecture that the Chicago School was trying to pioneer, unlike Sullivan the exposition was to be the starting point of Wright's career. Aside from the main Court of Honor buildings, there were exhibitions from all over the world and Wright almost certainly visited the pre-Columbian architecture of the reconstruction of the Mayan Nunnery at Uxmal and Japan's Ho-o-den exhibit, a half-scale reconstruction of a Fujiwara period temple.

Many commentators on Wright's work have pointed out the formal similarities between Wright's work and traditional Japanese architecture and art. In the first extensive publication of Wright's work, in 1900, Robert Spencer Jr. (1865–1953), a fellow Chicago architect with whom Wright shared both a studio and a love of oriental art, pointed out that, while Wright generally looked at nature for inspiration at first hand, he also looked to the Japanese artists as "interpreters of nature." In 1911 C.R. Ashbee, the English Arts and Crafts designer, pointed to a clear Japanese influence when he wrote

the introduction to the Wasmuth photo-study of Wright's work. Subsequent writers, such as the Dutch architect Hendrik Berlage and Henry Russell Hitchcock, have pointed out similar links between Wright's architecture and Japanese architectural forms and spaces. However Wright himself, throughout his entire career, was to deny strenuously any such direct influence. In 1957 he published *A Testament* in which he stated that the only influences—or at least the only ones he was prepared to acknowledge publicly—were the "Lieber Meister" (Louis Sullivan), Dankmar Adler, John Roebling (the architect of the Brooklyn Bridge in New York), Walt Whitman, and Ralph Waldo Emerson. In his book Wright wrote: "My work is original not only in fact but in spiritual fiber," although he did state that in the architecture of the Mayans and the Japanese he found, not inspiration, but confirmation of many of his ideas about organic architecture. Despite these and other documented denials, there is nonetheless the general notion that Wright did indeed owe a formal debt to these architectural examples.

Japanese Art and Architecture

At the close of the 19th century a general awareness of Japanese art was widespread among middle class Americans. For over two centuries the exclusion policy enforced by successive Japanese shoguns, which began in the 1630s with Iemitsu Tokugawa (1604–51), had effectively isolated Japan from the rest of the world. Consequently, apart from a small amount of trade with the Chinese, Portuguese, and later the Dutch, few Japanese products reached the west until 1854 when Commodore Matthew Perry (1794–1858) persuaded the Tokugawa government to open some Japanese ports to foreign ships.

The artistic benefits of the opening up of Japan were to be seen almost immediately in Europe: French graphic designer Felix Bracquemond is credited with the discovery

in 1856 of a copy of Hokusai's (1760–1849) *Manga*, a series of sketchbooks published over a 40-year period and containing illustrations of every conceivable natural and man-made object, creating a picture of life in Edo Japan, which was to prove very influential.

Bracquemond's discovery excited a great deal of interest in "Japonisme": exhibitions of Japanese goods were held in London (1862), Paris (1867), and Vienna (1873) and by the mid-1870s there was a steady flow of Japanese art and artefacts to Europe. The influence of these new discoveries on the visual arts was phenomenal and was to inspire many of the leading artists of the period: Manet, Degas, Toulouse-Lautrec, Gauguin, and Van Gogh, as well as American artists based in Europe like James McNeill Whistler and Mary Cassatt.

In America at this early stage, however, until the 1876 Philadelphia Centennial Exposition, interest in Japanese art was confined to a few artists and collectors in the major cities. We know that Wright's mother Anna definitely visited the exposition—it was here that she is reported to have discovered the Froebel educational "Gifts"—although it is not certain whether the nine-year old Wright accompanied her. The impact on both the general public and architects of the two Japanese buildings—a dwelling and a Japanese bazaar—was to be seen in domestic interior decoration in many homes, and in the construction of complete buildings in the Japanese manner. One of these was Bruce Price's Tuxedo Park resort development in the Catskill Mountains: it was designed on a Japanese theme as a weekend retreat for wealthy New Yorkers.

Wright's first direct experience of Japanese architecture came at the World's Columbian Exposition. The Ho-o-do temple

ABOVE RIGHT AND RIGHT: Pennsylvania station, New York, was another of the "American Renaissance" buildings of the time. Its huge waiting room was based on the tepidarium of the Baths of Caracalla in Rome—but was at least 25 percent bigger.

was originally built as part of the Byodo-in, a residential temple complex which had been the private home of the imperial regent Yorimichi Fujiwara (990–1074) until it was converted into a family temple in 1052. The Ho-o-do is considered by many as one of the definitive works of Japanese architecture and its reconstruction, albeit on a much smaller scale, at the World's Fair attracted a great deal of attention from the press, which described in great detail the Ho-o-den (the secular suffix den was applied to the Jackson Park reconstruction to distinguish it from its religious model, the Ho-o-do). It was the merging of religious and domestic forms in the building that appears to have made a lasting impression on Wright: throughout his subsequent career he treated the "institutions" of dwelling and temple as interchangeable, striving to make the home a spiritual place and the church a human one.

One of Wright's most important architectural innovations can also be traced back to the Ho-o-den: in his Prairie Houses he abandoned the conventional "box" containing smaller "boxes" created by fixed interior dividing walls that was the typical construction of American homes. From examination of this model, Wright was also to realize that the most efficient place to support a roof was not at its very edges (as in traditional European architecture) but slightly in at the corners, thereby allowing the roof to create a large overhang. The supporting structural members could now be the continuous wall or "panels" which Wright was to term "screens."

While the Ho-o-den was to be Wright's introduction to Japanese architecture, his interest in Japanese art in general, and in woodblock prints in particular, had developed prior to the World's Fair, while he was working for his first employer, Joseph Lyman Silsbee (1848–1913). Silsbee, like many aesthetically minded people at the time, was known to collect oriental *objets d'art*, although with regard to Japanese prints, he was an enthusiastic amateur.

More important in the field of Japanese art scholarship was Silsbee's cousin, Ernest Fenellosa (1853–1908), who was the first foreigner to survey Japanese temple art and was to become one of the leading authorities in the field. So influential was Fenellosa that he played a leading role within Japan itself in preventing the study and practice of traditional art forms from disappearing from the Japanese educational system. Decorated by the Emperor Meiji for his services to education, Fenellosa was appointed to the Imperial Fine Arts Commission which, in 1886, went on a fact-finding tour of western art institutions. By the time Fenellosa and the commission arrived in America in October 1886, Silsbee had already known Wright for two years, and by early 1887 Wright was employed in Silsbee's Chicago office. It appears that Fenellosa did visit his cousin during his tour but, once again, whether Wright met with him is a mystery. What is certain is that by the early 1890s Wright was well aware of Fenellosa's work; it even seems that the first prints in Wright's collection were obtained through Fenellosa.

In his efforts to educate westerners in the aesthetics of traditional Japanese pictorial art, Fenellosa developed a theory which was eventually turned into a practical course of art instruction by his friend, the painter and teacher Arthur Dow (1865–1922). Dow's book *Composition*, published in 1899, was to have a major impact on the teaching of art in American schools in the first part of the 20th century and, it seems, on the work of Wright. Like Fenellosa, Dow regarded all the visual arts as "space-arts" which were concerned with essentially the same thing: the aesthetic division of space. In *Composition*, Dow illustrated this concept in a series of simple patterns or what he termed "synthetic line-ideas" to demonstrate how the lines created

a mutually interdependent organic whole. Shortly after the appearance of Dow's *Composition*, Wright was to design his "Home in a Prairie Town" project for the *Ladies' Home Journal* which was based on a cruciform of four interlocking rectangles reminiscent of Dow's "line-ideas."

Dow also maintained that the basic elements of design were line, color, and *notan*, the Japanese term for the arrangement of light and dark. Both Fenellosa and Dow believed that creativity, regardless of medium, could emerge not from the literal representation of objects, but from mastery of the principles of composition. Dow's book used numerous Japanese examples to demonstrate how, in the oriental aesthetic of "rhythm and harmony," modeling and the imitation of nature were subordinate. This was an approach which both Sullivan and Wright would come to share.

In 1890 Fenellosa was in charge of the newly established Japanese art department at the Boston Museum of Fine Art and lectured widely on the aesthetic principles of Japanese art. This, he believed, could become the basis of a new, truly American, art which was finally independent of European models and traditions. For these ideas Fenellosa found a particularly receptive audience in Chicago. In 1893 he was a lecturer and judge at the World's Fair and, in 1894, Wright's friend and fellow Japanese print collector Frederick Gookin (1853–1936) sponsored a series of Fenellosa's lecturers at the Art Institute of Chicago.

From the time of his initial contact with Joseph Silsbee and his own first visit to Japan in 1905, Wright had undoubtedly become familiar with Fenellosa's ideas on Japanese art and how its aesthetic principles could be applied in America, particularly in architecture. This, coupled with Fenellosa's criticisms of European architectural traditions being "transplanted" in cultures outside Europe, most certainly made a great impression on Frank Lloyd Wright.

ABOVE: JAPONAISERIE—BRIDGE IN THE RAIN (AFTER HIROSHIGE). Van Gogh's late 1887 painting typifies the influence of Japanese art on European painters.

BELOW: VARIATIONS IN FLESH COLOR AND GREEN—THE BALCONY. American-born James McNeill Whistler painted this Japanese-influenced image 1864–70.

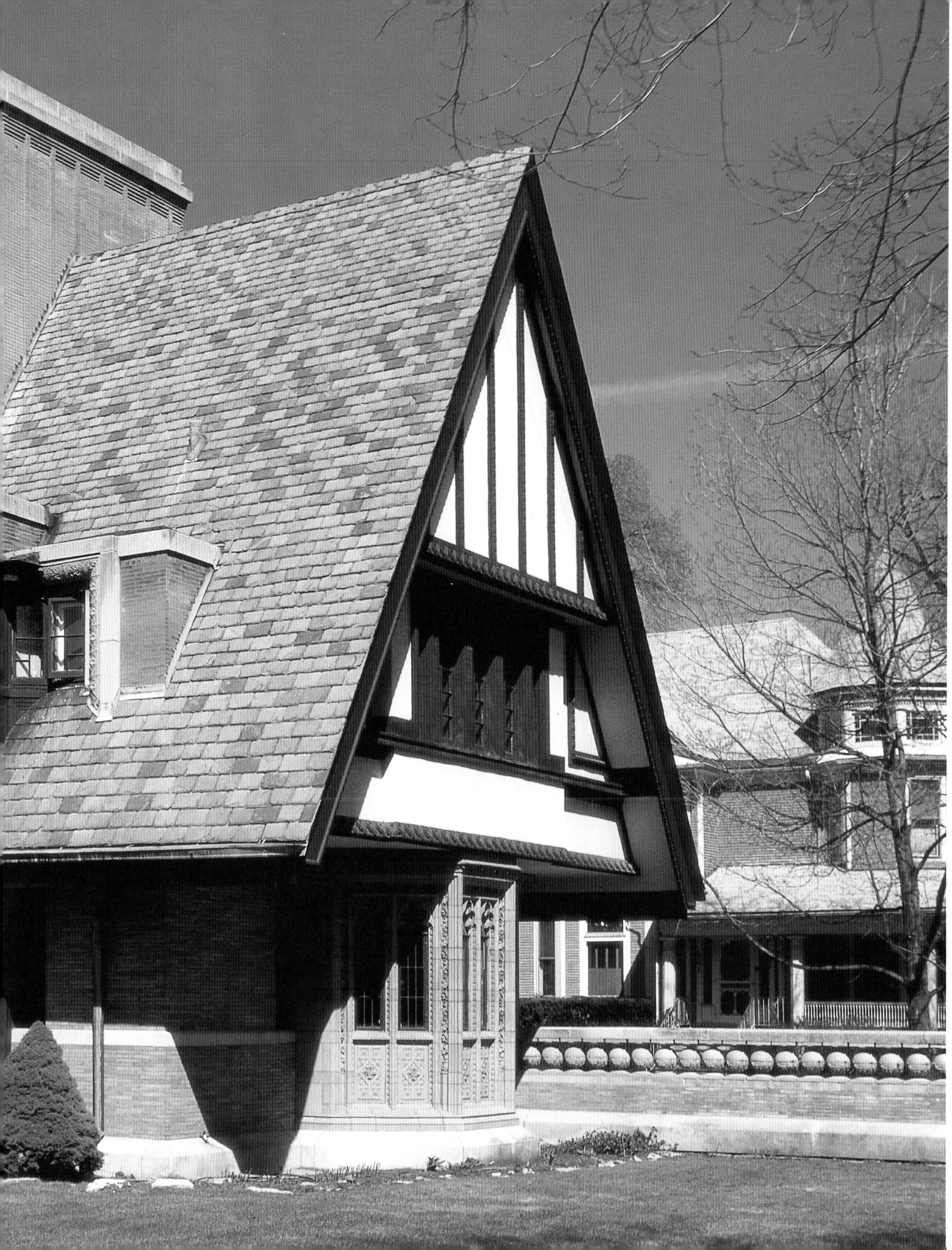

LEARNING HIS TRADE

LEARNING HIS TRADE

The exact date of Wright's arrival in Chicago is not known, but from his autobiography, and from records at the University of Wisconsin where he had been enrolled as a special student, it seems that it was some time in the spring of 1887 that Wright left Madison to begin his architectural career in the offices of Joseph Lyman Silsbee.

An easterner by birth, Silsbee was regarded as one of the finest architects in Chicago. He designed and built houses in the "Shingle" style, a style derived from the English architect Norman Shaw and which had already proved popular on the east coast of America. By 1887 Silsbee was a much sought-after architect for houses and related buildings such as clubs. At this time Silsbee was also working on an important project, the development of Edgewater, a new lakeside suburb development for J.L. Cochrane on the northern edge of Chicago. A second commission came from the Reverend Jenkin Lloyd Jones, Wright's uncle, to design a new meeting house for All Souls Church which had grown from its origins in a grocery store to a congregation large and rich enough to be able to finance the construction of a new church. Jenkin Lloyd Jones had been attracted by Silsbee's Shingle style houses and it was a "home" for the congregation, rather than a church in the usual sense, that he sought.

Wright had knowledge of this commission before he had left Madison for Chicago and, although he wrote in his autobiography that he did not want to use the "family connection," he knew that he had, at least, one foot in the door. Appointed as a draftsman, Wright reported for work the next day and All Souls became the first piece of architecture in which Frank Lloyd Wright was

actively engaged. Uncle Jenkin's determination that the building should have a homely feel made the building appear more like a suburban clubhouse than a church; like the Edgewater development houses, it was made of a mixture of bricks and brown shingles.

The first instance of the "hand" of Silsbee's new young draftsman appears in published drawings for J.L. Cochrane's house in the Edgewater development: the pen and ink perspective is inscribed in the corner "Frank Lloyd Wright, Del." ("Del" for "delineator.") The projects for Silsbee, it appears, were not enough for the eager and ambitious Wright and independently he undertook four projects dating from this period.

In 1887 Wright designed a small Unitarian Chapel for a congregation in Sioux City, Iowa. The chapel bears a marked

PREVIOUS PAGE: THE MOORE HOUSE (1895) was in a "mock Tudor" style he disliked, but it enhanced Wright's growing reputation for residential design nevertheless.

BELOW: Detail from Owen Jones's book, *The Grammar of Ornament* (1856).

resemblance to the Jones's All Souls Church: it is a picturesque stone and shingle structure with a conical tower and an informal floor plan. The simple, one-room interior can be subdivided by moveable screens for social gatherings. At one end of the room is a fireplace; at the other, a speaker's platform. A small recess serves as the pastor's study area, which is balanced on the other side by a circular alcove topped by a cupola. No mention is made of this chapel, Wright's first independent commission, in his autobiography: it appears that Wright was ashamed of it and called it his *bête noire*. Wright disliked being seen to have "borrowed" any elements or styles from identifiable predecessors.

Also in 1887 Wright undertook a commission for his maiden aunts, the Misses Jane and Nell Lloyd Jones. This was to be the first building for Hillside Home School at Spring Green, Wisconsin. The Misses Jones had promised never to marry, and to dedicate their lives to their school; whenever the school needed new buildings, the aunts called on their nephew. The Hillside Home project was to continue sporadically into the opening years of the 20th century but it undoubtedly began at a time when Wright was under Silsbee's supervision, since the general effect of the roofs and gables are once again in Silsbee's Shingle style.

In addition to the Sioux City chapel project, there are two further published drawings by Wright from his earliest period: Country Residence I and II for Hillside Estate. Both of these designs were published in the *Inland Architect and News Record*, the first in August 1887, the second in February 1888. It seems that these schemes were for the development of Lloyd Jones family land. The drawings are annotated with the location of

Silsbee introduced to the Chicago area the fashion from the east for the "Colonial" style of architecture. Wright no doubt was watching his former employer's actions very closely, for by 1894 Wright himself had erected two houses in the Colonial manner: the Blossom House and the Bagley House.

In late fall 1887 Wright applied to the office of Sullivan and Adler for a position of draftsman. An interview was arranged and Wright stayed up for three nights preparing drawings to take along: some were re-workings of Silsbee's drawings for ornament, others were Gothic ornaments from Owen Jones's book that Wright admitted he made look more like Sullivan's own drawing style. Sullivan evidently studied the drawings dur-

LEFT, RIGHT, AND BELOW: THE CHARNLEY HOUSE (1891), Chicago, Illinois. Wright called the Charnley townhouse "the first modern building" and in it he said he first recognized the decorative value of plain surfaces. It was the first great building of his career but still owes a great deal to to his "Lieber Meister": the open second-story loggia (Left) was a favorite Sullivan device and in details such as in the decorative carving of the woodwork of the stairwell, the influence of Louis Sullivan is clearly evident.

Helena Valley, Wisconsin—an area which no longer exists but can be found on contemporary maps of Wisconsin. It appears that the Lloyd Joneses wished to give their young relative every encouragement in his career and possibly be responsible for his debut as an architect independent of Silsbee. However, the designs for Country Residences I and II are very much in the spirit of Silsbee's Edgewater projects.

Wright was to remain in Silsbee's offices for a mere seven or eight months, up to the fall of 1887. During his stay, Wright began his first serious study of architecture and its history. Over 100 tracings from Owen Jones's *The Grammar of Ornament* and Viollet-le-Duc's *Dictionnaire Raisonné* date from this period. Nevertheless, Wright began to feel restless and eager to move on, but he was never to forget Silsbee and traces of his influence remained in Wright's work throughout the 1890s, just after he began to practice independently. Just before 1890

ing the interview and, despite his caustic comments, Wright was hired at $25 a week.

When Wright reported for work at his new employers, Sullivan and Adler were engaged on the design for the Auditorium Building. Wright's career at Sullivan and Adler was one of rapid rise: when he first joined the firm, it was housed on the top floor of the Borden Block in Randolph Street in Chicago—a building designed by Sullivan and Adler in 1880. By the time the Auditorium Building was completed in 1889, the firm had moved into new headquarters in the loft of the great tower. Here Wright had his own office—next to, and the same size as, Sullivan's.

Among his numerous responsibilities were commissions for private houses. Sullivan and Adler were, on the whole, not interested in domestic architecture but were often under pressure from clients and their friends to design residences. These the firm undertook for diplomatic reasons but they

were largely passed over to Wright. It is now well accepted that the houses erected by Sullivan and Adler after 1887 were the work of Wright and were designed at home after normal business hours. From 1887 to 1893, the period of Wright's employment at Sullivan and Adler, the firm built nine houses. The two completed in 1887 must have been under way well before Wright arrived, but from the beginning of 1888 it appears that Wright was firmly in control of the domestic commissions.

Although officially a Sullivan and Adler design, the Charnley House in Astor Street, Chicago, built in 1891 is, in reality, the first great building of Wright's career. The Charnleys were personal friends of Sullivan—they had bought adjacent parcels of land in Ocean Springs near Biloxi in Mississippi. Sullivan had been under increasing strain during the construction of the Auditorium Building and the house he

intended to build on the Gulf of Mexico was to be used as a retreat. A similar cottage was to be built on the Charnleys' land next door. It is possible that Sullivan drew quick sketches for the Charnleys and then, once these had been approved, they were turned over to Wright to complete. Wright himself called the Charnley townhouse "the first modern building" and in it he said he first recognized the decorative value of plain surfaces. Nevertheless, the Charnley House owes a great deal to Sullivan: the open second-story loggia was a favorite device of Sullivan's and was used by him on the Auditorium Building and the Schiller Building. Sullivan also favored arches: inside, on the ground floor, there are six, but the most Sullivanesque touches are in the decorative detailing on the wood trim throughout the house. The plan of the house is simple: a stair hall in the center rises to the top of the building and is flanked on each floor by two rooms. The kitchen, as

was usual for townhouses built in cramped city lots, was located in the basement.

Around the time of the Charnley House, the plans for the Transportation Building for the Chicago World's Fair had been completed by the firm. By this stage Wright was Sullivan's "right-hand man." The construction of the building, which presented engineering problems, was largely the work of Dankmar Adler, but the great portal, the building's most famous feature, was the work of Sullivan and Wright. The Transportation Building was essentially a large empty hall to be filled with exhibits of locomotives and the new "horseless carriages." Once the structure had been resolved, the building was to be "attractively clothed" in the classical style dictated by the organizing committee of architects: all the buildings were to have a cornice at a prescribed 60-foot height and, if they were not cast in the classical style, they were to have

LEFT: THE BLOSSOM HOUSE (1892), Chicago, Illinois. One of Wright's bootlegged houses, this was his only working of New England "Colonial," a style that had been made popular in the Midwest by architects such as Joseph Lyman Silsbee.

RIGHT: THE WALTER GALE HOUSE (1893), Oak Park, Illinois. Another of the 10 bootlegged commissions, the Walter Gale House bears traces of an earlier project during his period of employment with Silsbee—the project for All Souls' Church. The huge polygonal windows are evidence of Wright's increasing interest in the ways in which rooms could be opened up—if not to each other, then to the outside.

running arcades. Within these restrictions, Sullivan and Adler managed to create the most striking building at the fair and its central portal, the "Golden Gate" with its Oriental touches and rich surface ornament, was its greatest achievement.

As has been described in the last chapter, the Chicago World's Fair was important to Wright for a second reason. It was there on the "Wooded Isle," a small plot of land set in an artificial lake and approached by a bridge, that the Ho-o-den had been erected as the official exhibit of the Imperial Japanese government. The first large-scale introduction to the Midwest of Japanese art and architecture, for Wright it was a confirmation of his early interest in Oriental art. Despite Wright's constant denials throughout his career that Japanese architecture played any role in influencing his own, there are certainly affinities between the structure of the Ho-o-den and Wright's later concepts of interior space.

The central hall of the Ho-o-den had no solid walls, only posts and sliding screens, which could be used to change the appearance of the room depending on the activities taking place therein. The temple opened outwards towards the paper windows. These were fitted into slots that could be removed when not needed, opening up the interior space onto the gardens. Daylight entered through the continuous band of windows but glare was reduced by the overhang of the roof eaves. In the Ho-o-den Wright discovered a new architecture which came close to his own ideas and would be developed in the Prairie House.

In 1889 Wright's association with Sullivan and Adler was formalized by the drawing-up of a five-year binding contract. Wright had met Catherine Tobin and wanted to marry her. But above all else he wanted to build his own house, and the contract gave him the means to fulfil his ambitions. Under its terms Wright was able to draw advances on his salary to meet his new obligations—but it was not long before he found himself in financial difficulties, something that would

burden him throughout his career. Faced with mounting debts and an increasing family—within a year of marriage a first child, Frank Lloyd Wright Junior, was born—Wright took on commissions for houses "on the side." The nine or ten buildings—ten were designed, nine were built—from this period, undertaken when he was employed by Sullivan and Adler, Wright called his "bootlegged" houses. While these commissions were not really in violation of his contract of

employment, Wright nevertheless regarded them as somewhat clandestine, since he never mentioned their existence to his employer and even went as far to have some of them announced in contractor's journals as the work of his friend Cecil Corwin.

The bootlegged houses were all built or projected by the late spring of 1893. The 10 houses were for: Dr. A.W. Harlan in Chicago (1891); W.S. MacHarg, Chicago (1891); Warren McArthur, Chicago (1892); George Blossom, Chicago (1892); Robert Emmond, LaGrange, Illinois (1892); two identical houses for Thomas H. Gale, Oak Park, Chicago (1892); Walter Gale, Oak Park (1893); Orrin S. Goan, LaGrange (designed 1893 but not built); Peter Goan, LaGrange (1893).

In his autobiography Wright apologized for the appearance of the bootlegged houses and claimed that they looked the way they did because he was unable to supervise their construction personally. But while he claimed they were influenced by Sullivan, in fact they bore more obviously a debt to Silsbee. Most of his clients had come under the spell of Silsbee's style and any innovations that Silsbee had introduced were more

ABOVE: FRANK LLOYD WRIGHT HOME AND STUDIO (1889–1911), Oak Park, Illinois. With a loan from Louis Sullivan, in 1889 Wright began the construction of his own house. It would serve as his showpiece and his workshop: from 1899 to 1909 it would always be in a state of flux as new ideas were put into practice. At the left of the picture is Wright's studio and drafting room—an octagonally roofed two-story structure added in 1898, the octagon on a cube again recalling his early childhood experience of the Froebel "Gifts." The exterior of the house reflects Wright's interest in the Shingle style of architecture popular on the East Coast at the time.

likely to be accepted than those by the young and unknown Wright. Silsbee had already introduced the Colonial style of domestic architecture in the Midwest; Wright's only work in the revived New England Colonial style was the Blossom House, complete with yellow clapboards, white trim, classical portico, fan-lighted doorway, and Palladian windows. Yet there are already Wrightian touches evident in the low hip roof, the projection of the eaves (which replace the traditional classical cornice) and the massive Roman brick chimney. Next door, its neighbor the McArthur house reworks the Dutch Colonial style. The McArthur house was Wright's opportunity to design not only the building but all of its fittings and some of its furniture. For the first time in his career, Wright was able to put into

practice his belief that it was the duty of the architect to carry a design to its ultimate conclusion. Inside, the woodwork of the hall and dining room, the built-in buffet, and the glazed interior doors are a hint of Wright's work to come in later masterpieces like the Robie House.

The pair of houses for Thomas Gale, as well as the Goan and Emmond houses, are all plain frame structures. The Walter Gale house has a two-story, semicircular bay, which is reminiscent of Silsbee's design for All Souls Church. The other houses in this group share a common plan: along one side of the building are three rooms, the front, and back parlors, and the dining room; along the other side are the stairs, the kitchen, and storage closets. This plan was a practical solution for a small house of the period but one which Wright, with his increasing interest in interior space, must have found very dated. Nevertheless, in his desire to "bring the outside inside," he did add the oversized, glazed corner polygons. Inside, the great bays take up most of the wall space while outside they are capped by tall, pointed, polygonal roofs. The house for W.S. MacHarg

Three more views of Wright's Home and Studio. The interior spaces of the house are open—Wright disliked the concept of the house as a box containing smaller boxes—and the fixtures and furnishings were conceived as part of the overall plan.

ABOVE: The living room.

ABOVE RIGHT: The barrel-vaulted playroom

BELOW: The two-story octagonal drafting room.

has long since been demolished and it is known only by a single photograph. It appears to have been a clapboard house of two and a half storys, covered with a high-pitched hip roof.

The Harlan House was the most radical of the bootlegged houses in elevation and plan and its low hip roof is characteristic of the next phase in Wright's career. Inside it was originally one long rectangle but, at the client's insistence, the inner space was bisected with an inner partition to create twin parlors. The main feature of the Harlan interior is its stair hall: a two-story well of open design with the staircase rising at one corner. On the oblong newel-post are Sullivanesque ornaments of curling foliage and arabesques of interlaced lines.

The bootlegged commissions were not the only projects occupying Wright's time during his stay with Sullivan and Adler. In addition to the work on his own house at Oak Park, Wright entered and won, an architectural competition sponsored by the Madison Improvement Association in February 1893 for the design of the Municipal Boathouse on the shores of Lake

Mendota in Madison, Wisconsin. $4,000 was allotted for the building and Wright's winning design was for a frame structure with shingle sides. The plan was based on a semicircle that terminated in square pavilions with a second-story promenade. Because of the sharply sloping site, visitors entered the boathouse at the upper level and descended to the boat moorings by stairs. The low-pitched roofs with their heavy overhang of eaves were by this stage becoming a familiar feature of Wright's work.

In the fall of 1889 Wright began to build his own house. He had bought Lot No. 20, a corner lot on the then un-named streets of Forest and Chicago Avenues, in the new Oak Park suburb in Cicero township. At the rear of the lot there already stood a small cottage, which, when renovated, was to become home for Wright's mother Anna for many years. Like his later homes, Taliesin North and Taliesin West, the Oak Park home and studio, continually underwent enlargement but, in its original state, it was a modest house with a steep triangular roof with projecting eaves set on the low walls of the rectangular base of the house. Inside the house there was little of the later "decompartmentalizing" of space. Instead there are the Silsbee-style polygonal bays and inglenooks.

In 1893 Wright and Sullivan parted company and Wright's center of activity became Oak Park—although he kept an office in Chicago for meetings with clients. Around 1894 Wright made his first alterations to his house by adding a barrel-ceilinged playroom at the back of the second floor. This became the space for the neighborhood kindergarten, which Wright's wife Catherine directed, and a "concert" space for the family—Wright encouraged all his children to learn at least one musical instrument. Over the fireplace were painted scenes from the Arabian Nights and there were chandeliers of cubes and globes wired for electricity.

In 1895 Wright negotiated a contract with the American Luxfer Prism Company, a scheme designed to bring more light into deep rooms or businesses by adding prismatic lenses in bands on the upper panels of windows. This brought him extra money to add a workshop on the Chicago Avenue side of the house: this became known as the "Studio." Additions to the studio were continuous: it was a "laboratory" of ideas. The drafting room, a vertical space lit from above encircled by a balcony, is a form that Wright adopted for many of the large public commissions: Unity Temple, the Larkin

BELOW: In sharp contrast to the Winslow House (RIGHT), the sharply pitched roof and dormer windows of the Williams House (1895) is more in the manner of Silsbee.

Administration Building, the Johnson Wax Administration Building, and the Guggenheim Museum.

Independent of Sullivan and Adler, Wright began to concentrate on developing the principles of his architecture. Soon after he and his colleague Cecil Corwin rented office space in the Schiller Building, William H. Winslow came to commission a new house in River Forest, a new suburb to the west of Oak Park. Winslow was a businessman and president of a large manufacturer of ornamental ironwork. He had enjoyed a long and close business relationship with Sullivan and Adler and, knowing that this firm was not interested in domestic commissions, appears to have turned to Wright despite the fact that he was only 24 years old. Winslow's

plot of land on Auvergne Place was on a private street on the Waller Estate. Edward Waller was a highly successful entrepreneur in Chicago and an admirer of Wright: he had Wright remodel his dining room in his (now demolished) house which was opposite Winslow's and commissioned a house from him that was never built.

The Winslow House was to be Wright's first important independent commission and hints at the Prairie Houses to come. The most striking aspect of the Winslow House is the broad-eaved hip roof that is uninterrupted by the usual dormer windows. There is also the optical illusion created by the door, which appears to be smaller than it actually is. The outer walls of the building are made of a lower band of Roman brick and an upper band of tiles. The dark orange brick, bronze-glazed tiles, buff-colored limestone and terracotta roof tiles give a warm, fall-like color to the house. From a short distance, the band of tiles appears only as a neutral tone, differentiating the second story from the lower one. Close to, we see the

Sullivanesque ornament of the tiles but handled by Wright in a more geometric manner. The broken surface of the decorative tiles fractures the light and sets up a play of shadows which makes the wall under the overhanging eaves appear lighter and less solid than it actually is. (This was a device that Wright had, no doubt, learned from Sullivan, who was also to use ornament for a similar effect in the Carson-Pirie-Scott Store of 1899.)

On the north side of the Winslow House is a feature that was indispensable to elegant living: a *porte-cochère*, under which one parked and descended from an automobile. The spandrels of the arched *porte-cochère* are again carved in leafy Sullivanesque motifs. The east (or rear) facade contrasts strongly with the front (west) facade: there is a projecting wing and a tall polygonal stair-tower.

Winslow may have been a businessman but his hobbies were printing and typography. One of the stipulations for his house was that a studio and press room should be incorporated into the stable block

at the rear of the house. The stable in its early years boasted a tree growing through its roof—a device that Wright delighted in and incorporated in his own house and in the Isabel Roberts House. In the Winslow stables, where the tree poked through, a rather crude gasket of rubber and cloth kept the roof from leaking. The stable block gave Winslow ample room—if somewhat leaky—for his work on the Auvergne Press which published finely produced, hand-set, limited editions of books. One of the Auvergne Press products was *The House Beautiful* by William C. Gannet, a Unitarian minister admired by both Wright and Winslow. Gannet believed that the home was the center of family love, virtue, and culture and that houses should be well constructed, well ventilated, well lit, and sanitary. Wright designed Gannet's book, drew individual page decorations, and even wrote the preface for it. Copies of the finished books were given away to friends and colleagues.

Not everyone thought the Winslow House to be a masterpiece: following the completion of the house William Winslow underwent some mild persecution and for a few months he avoided traveling to and from his Chicago office on his regular morning and evening train so that he didn't have to put up with the remarks of his fellow commuters. Despite the notoriety of the Winslow House, Wright continued to receive commissions for other houses in the Oak Park and River Forest areas. But not all his clients wanted something new and different: at the same time as Wright was supervising the Winslow house he was working on a house for Chauncey Williams, one block east of Auvergne Place. A complex of angles and a sharply pitched, overhanging roof, with odd dormers that intersect it, the design is a picturesque Silsbee-style house that contrasts sharply with the Winslow House.

One client, Nathan Moore, came to Wright in late 1894 with the commission for an "English House." It transpired that Moore wanted a mock Tudor half-timbered black-and-white house. At first Wright contemplated the idea of simply remodeling Moore's existing old frame house in Forest Avenue, directly opposite his own studio. Although elaborate plans (now lost, but still referred to as Moore House I) were drawn up, the idea was abandoned. Moore House II was built without reference to the existing building and was completed in 1895. It was gutted by fire in 1922 and Moore contacted Wright, who had just returned from Japan, and a new enlarged Moore House II was built on the same foundations. Just to complicate matters further, the original frame building that Wright had earlier contemplated remodeling was moved to the south edge of the property to make room for the first Moore House II. In 1900 the original frame building was remodeled. This building still stands and is known as Moore House III. Exactly why

Moore approached Wright to design him a Tudor style house is not known, as Wright had no experience in this style—it may simply have been a matter of convenience as Wright and Moore were such close neighbors. One result was that Wright had to fend off clients who wanted Tudor style Moore Houses for several years.

Nevertheless, experience with the Tudor style led Wright to experiment with it again in the four party-wall Roloson Houses, a commission unique in Wright's work. It came in 1894 from Robert Roloson, who happened to be a son-in-law of Edward Waller and who owned some property on the south side of Chicago that he wished to improve. The idea was to erect a row of four identical houses to be rented out and provide a return on the investment. The modified Tudor style houses designed by Wright were conceived on a mezzanine plan: there is a break in the floor level at the central stair well and the rooms to the rear of the stairs are several steps lower than those in the front. Interior spaces constantly shift as the floor heights vary and the main rooms are separated from each other by smaller "introductory" rooms. Outside, the front of the Roloson Houses is dominated by the four great gables and the only applied ornament is in the three square spandrels on each facade. In front of each house is a paved terrace approached by a flight of three steps. Separating the terraces from the sidewalk are balustrades decorated with Sullivanesque patterns.

Despite increasing success and recognition, there were still disappointments for Wright. There were several commissions which were never to get beyond the project stage, such as the planned houses for Edward Waller, Warren Furbeck, Jesse Baldwin, Henry Cooper, C.H. McAfee, and Mrs. David Devlin.

RIGHT: THE ROMEO AND JULIET WINDMILL (1896), Spring Green, Wisconsin. One of Wright's smallest commissions, the windmill was built for his aunts Nell and Jane Lloyd Jones to provide water for their experimental Hillside Home School.

One project which, compared to the Winslow or Roloson Houses, was small in size and cost less than $1,000 but which nevertheless remained of great personal significance to Wright, was the commission from his maiden aunts Nell and Jane Lloyd Jones for the Romeo and Juliet Windmill at the Hillside Home School. In 1895, to ensure an adequate water supply to the school, a reservoir was dug out of solid rock at the top of the hill behind the school. To pump water out of an artesian well into the reservoir the aunts had first proposed buying a metal windmill but it occurred to them that their nephew might be able to build them something more in keeping with their aesthetic ideas. When Wright's design arrived at Hillside, the local builder was appalled, convinced that the windmill would fall over in the first storm. An octagonal turret, 60ft high, capped by a disc and containing a circular staircase, the windmill was to be made of timber and shingles. The builder and Wright's five uncles, whose own properties had an unobstructed view of the structure and were convinced that a bought metal windmill would have been cheaper and more efficient, were outraged. Concerned, the aunts telegraphed Wright with the message: "Cramer [the local builder] says windmill tower sure to fall. Are you sure it will stand?" Wright's telegraphed reply was simply: "Build it." Wright was convinced that the windmill would stand for 25 years: today Romeo and Juliet Windmill still stands on the hill behind the Hillside Home School buildings, which are now used as the drafting rooms for the Taliesin Fellowship.

The windmill helped Wright establish credibility as an architect within his own family. The success of the windmill dispelled doubts in his uncles' minds, including those of his Uncle Jenkin who had once recommended that Wright did not go to Chicago to become an architect. Possibly because of the windmill, Jenkin Lloyd Jones commissioned his nephew to design a new church in

ABOVE: THE MOORE HOUSE (1895), Oak Park, Illinois. Not all his clients wanted a Winslow House and although Wright had no experience in building in the "mock Tudor" style, Nathan Moore, a close neighbor of Wright's, was eventually provided with one. Mock Tudor with a hint of Swiss chalet and Japonisme, Wright claimed that he undertook the commission because he needed the money and because he felt challenged by the opportunity to produce something in a style which he disliked intensely! To his complete horror, the Moore House proved popular and he had to turn away clients who wanted houses in the same style. He did, however, experiment with the style again in the Roloson Apartments, a row of four identical party-wall houses, dominated on the outside by four great gables.

Chicago to replace Silsbee's All Souls which his congregation had outgrown. The new church, the Abraham Lincoln Center, would also contain auditoria, meeting rooms, offices, kitchens, a gym, and living quarters for Uncle Jenkin and family. At street level there were also to be retail shops, the rents

from which would support the church. Wright set about the designs and produced models for his uncle, but none pleased him and the pair clashed repeatedly. Finally, in 1902, Wright turned the project over to his colleague Dwight Perkins after scribbling on the blueprints: "bldg. completed over protest of architect." The Abraham Lincoln Center finally opened in 1905 and bore little resemblance to any of Wright's plans and is never included in any list of Wright's completed works.

In the last years of the 19th century Wright was commissioned by Isidore Heller and Joseph Husser to design and build houses for them in Chicago. The Heller House (1896) still stands but the Husser House

LEFT: THE ABRAHAM LINCOLN CENTER (1903), Chicago, Illinois. Wright's son John Lloyd claims the original design for this building was his father's first architectural work and should be dated 1888. Originally intended as a community center when the Reverend Jenkin Lloyd Jones commissioned it, the building was finally built in a changed form in 1903.

(1899), which looked out over Lake Michigan before apartment buildings hemmed it in, was demolished.

The Heller House is long and narrow with a "monitor" roof—a third, smaller, story is added above the main eaves and is capped with its own roof. The walls of the third story, which is only partly enclosed, are decorated with a frieze of foliate ornaments broken by open arcades. The human figures carved in high relief, which are the central feature of each panel of the frieze, were the work of Oak Park sculptor Richard Bock, who was to collaborate with Wright on many commissions. The main door of the house is a square opening, flanked on either side by Romanesque columns. Above the entrance, at the second story level, is an inset porch with a row of filigreed terracotta columns which support the load above it.

The Husser House was the last commission where the influence of Louis Sullivan on ornamentation would be so apparent: the second-story windows set in arcades resembled minor versions of the arches of the Golden Doors of the Transportation Building. But it would also point the way forward towards the houses of Wright's First Golden Age in its centrifugal plan—a forerunner of the "pinwheel" and "windmill" plans of later works—and in its scheme of a raised basement. Placing the basement at ground level meant that it was no longer a basement but became the area for "secondary activities" in the house: servant's rooms, entry halls, children's play areas, and laundry areas. The main areas of the living rooms and dining room were thereby raised above their more usual level to a quieter, elevated position which gave (then) open views across the landscape and Lake Michigan.

Haute Trust Company of Indiana, were widely admired and often imitated. Wide sash windows and broad bays allowed in sunlight and air, while bands of ornament ran across the cornice and basement course. The Francisco Terrace, a 44-unit building also from 1895, is in a different class. These apartments were located in the low-income, densely populated area of Chicago known as the "Near West Side." The idea was that each pair of apartments should have direct access to the outdoors and did away with inner public corridors. The street front apartments were approached directly from the sidewalk, while those inside, facing onto the rectangular central courtyard, were reached via a single wide archway opening from the street. At each corner of the courtyard were open towers containing public stairways to the second

LEFT AND BELOW: THE HELLER HOUSE (1896), Chicago, Illinois. The "monitor" roof—a third, smaller, story—is added above the main eaves. The walls of the third story, which is only partly enclosed, are decorated with a frieze of foliate ornaments broken by open arcades. The decorative third-story figures (BELOW) are sculpted by Richard Bock, a regular contributor to Wright's buildings.

Bedrooms were located on the third story, corresponding roughly to where the attics would have been. Therefore, because the house did not have to accommodate any additional height under its roof, the whole three-story building was lower in height than the more usual two-and-a-half story houses, allowing for an increased horizontality.

Two other projects from this period were concerned not with individual dwellings but with mass housing: the Francis Apartments, erected in Chicago by the Terre

floor. From the stairs, access to the upper level apartments was via an overhanging walkway that ran along all four sides of the courtyard. Initially, Francisco Terrace was occupied solely by young, childless couples and was nicknamed "Honeymoon Court." The fact that there were no children playing in the central courtyard no doubt meant that the buildings were, at this time, relatively quiet and the only noise would have been the echoes of footsteps on the walkways.

After years of neglect, Francisco Terrace was demolished in 1974 in spite of attempts by local people to save it. The archway in cut stone and terracotta and the stairwell motifs were, however, saved. These were dismantled and reconstructed in Oak Park, at the entrance to a building on Euclid Place and Lake Street which has a similar exterior design, yet is smaller in scale and plan than the original Francisco Terrace building.

In addition to these domestic commissions, Wright also undertook several projects for public structures during this early period: the Wolf Lake and Cheltenham Beach resorts, the Mozart Gardens, the competition design for a bank sponsored by the magazine *Brickbuilder*, the office building for the American Luxfer Prism Company, and the long-demolished River Forest Golf Club.

The River Forest Golf Club of 1898 was the only clubhouse Wright designed in this early period but it was a forerunner of several to come. The central feature of the building was the large octagonal common room which was added when the club was enlarged in 1901. From this central room wings extended forwards and sideways, turning back on themselves and enclosing two small courtyards. With its very low, widely overhanging hip roofs, ribbon windows, and bands of masonry and shingle, the River Forest Clubhouse was the closest Wright got to the Prairie House in this early period.

The unexecuted designs from 1898 for the remodeling of the Mozart Gardens, a "road house" popular with cyclists, included a large barrel-vaulted room whose design was very similar to the top-floor dining room of Sullivan and Adler's hotel in the Auditorium Building. The Wolf Lake resort was intended as a large public pleasure ground along the shores of a shallow lake on the borders of Illinois and Indiana a few miles to the southeast of Chicago. Wright's unbuilt designs show a complex of buildings in semicircular arrangement linked by a succession of arches. Rising at regular intervals would have been geometric towers of the sort that Wright would later use in the Midway Gardens and in the Imperial Hotel. Similar to Wolf Lake, the Cheltenham Beach resort project for the shore of Lake Michigan at 79th Street was to be yet another unbuilt Edward Waller scheme, designed to compete with the existing Manhattan Beach resort.

The design for the Village Bank for the competition in *Brickbuilder* in 1894 consisted of a cube lighted by two sets of clerestory windows, a device favored by Wright for rooms which required uniform light and continuous wall space. Also from the same year is the projected office building for the American Luxfer Prism Company. The company wanted to popularize the use of its prismatic glass bricks as replacements for traditional glazed windows in commercial structures like offices and factories. The headquarters which Wright designed for them was to be a 10-story building, the facade of which was to be filled with 48 squares of prismatic glass—a building that was remarkably close to modern glass-box office buildings. Shortly after designing the building, Wright negotiated a contract with the company to act as their architectural consultant.

RIGHT: Francisco Terrace was a 44-unit apartment building built in 1895. All that remains of it is this entrance arch which bears traces of Sullivanesque foliate decoration. It was reconstructed in Oak Park in 1977. Francisco Terrace was Wright's third venture into mass housing: the Roloson Apartment Houses and the Francis Apartments all date from this early period.

THE PRAIRIE HOUSE

THE PRAIRIE HOUSE

In his studio at Oak Park Wright tested his ideas on the use of space to achieve a flowing unified effect and the Prairie House was planned. From the numerous commissions that came into the practice in 1900, the Ward Willits House in Highland Park of 1902 is claimed to be the first Prairie House to be designed. There was a delay of several years before the actual building of the Willits House, however, and the first Prairie Houses to be erected may well have been those for Warren Hickox and Harley Bradley, both in Kankakee, Illinois.

There is no doubt surrounding the date of the drawings for two model houses made by Wright in 1900 for the Curtis Publishing Company of Philadelphia. They received nation-wide publicity when they were published in the *Ladies' Home Journal* in February and July of 1901. The houses were part of a project launched a year earli-er by the president of Curtis Publishing, Edward Bok, whose aim was to improve the design of American houses, particularly with regard to sanitation and efficiency. Like William C. Gannet, the author of *The House Beautiful*, a book which Wright had designed and illustrated for Winslow's Auvergne Press in 1897, Bok was a champion of hygiene in the home and believed strongly in airy sleeping porches, sanitary bathrooms and kitchens, and servants quarters of a humane size.

Bok invited numerous architects to contribute designs, to be published in the *Journal*, of houses that could be constructed at a price that was within reach of its readers. A complete set of working drawings for the houses would be offered for public sale at a mere $5 per set. Many architects refused Bok's invitation and claimed it was beneath their dignity to engage in such a venture.

Wright, however, jumped at the opportunity to demonstrate that the best quality housing could be available to the greatest number of people at the lowest cost possible. It was in these designs that Wright officially and publicly unveiled the Prairie House: the title of the first drawing published in February was "A Home in a Prairie Town." These are fully fledged Prairie Houses except that they do not include the leaded casement windows in order to keep the price down; there is no longer any trace of the influence of his "Lieber Meister," Louis Sullivan. Wright's two houses were scaled down to meet the included itemized budgets. The first house was costed at $7,000; the second design, which was called "A Small House with Lots of Room in It," was estimated at around $5,800.

In the plan of the first house, the interior partitions are reduced to a bare minimum and, where possible, replaced by head-

height screens which indicate, without actually fixing, the function of the space and how people might move through the spaces. The ground-floor plan is thus a single space in which the dining and living areas and a library are accommodated. An alternative sketch substitutes two bedrooms for the original balcony over the unified living area. In the second design, in place of the now customary low hip roofs, there are gables, a feature that would mark Wright's work until 1906: Wright appears to have recognized that the average homemaker was attached to this traditional pointed roof shape.

Despite the fact that the designs were published in a nationally read magazine, the general effect on American homemakers was not immediate: apart from one commission for the Sutton House at McCook in Nebraska, no commissions came into the studio as a direct result of the publication of the drawings and the *Ladies' Home Journal* designs essentially remained paper plans.

Although Wright was still some years away from his first visit to Japan, he had already begun collecting Japanese prints and in 1900 the influence of Japanese art, if not architecture, was evident in his work. This is particularly true of the house and stable he designed for an attorney, S.A. Foster, in the new real estate development of West Pullman in the once open countryside to the southwest of Chicago. Foster was one of the financial backers of the West Pullman development and intended the house as a summer cottage. The vogue for Japonisme after the Philadelphia Centennial Exposition in 1876 and the Columbian World's Fair in Chicago in

1893 was especially strong in the design and decoration of summer resorts and houses across America. Inside the Foster House the plan is simple, with the fireplace serving as the main focus of the combined dining and living space. The bedrooms are lit by dormers which gently peak at the apex as does the gable roof.

In the Hickox and Bradley Houses, built in the same year, the Japanese influence is still evident but curiously mixed with a Swiss chalet style, that was also in vogue at the time, and the Tudor style that Wright had already employed in the black-and-white Moore House. The Hickox and Bradley Houses with their low, broad gables are also similar appearance to the design for "The Small House with Lots of Room in It" but both buildings were more "tailor-made" in

details and fixtures than the model house.

Following the Kankakee buildings, Wright designed two houses for his Oak Park friends Frank Thomas and Arthur Heurtley. As in the Husser House (1899), both the Thomas and the Heurtley Houses have their main rooms on the second floor, while the ground floor takes the place of the old-fashioned basement—a feature, like attics, that Wright disliked in traditional architecture. While the Husser House offered views over Lake Michigan, the two Oak Park houses were built on small plots of level land and only really have views of each other.

The Heurtley House uses a pinwheel plan in which the various elements "revolve" around a central hall within a rectilinear configuration. The principle was based on a natural growth pattern, the spiral, which in rec-

tilinear form becomes a pinwheel. The use of this technique is evidence of Wright's awareness of the structures in nature. The house has a broad sheltering roof—almost identical to the roofs of the Thomas and Winslow Houses—and orange-colored brick walls, which are laid in bands of regularly projecting and receding courses that create a strong horizontal effect. The front entrance is reached through a Romanesque arch similar to those entrance arches in the Thomas and Dana Houses. The horizontal theme is further accentuated by the screen-like windows, whose rhythm is punctuated by wooden mullions. Inside space is allowed to flow

continuously in the L-shape formed by the living and dining areas, both of which are linked to the hall at first-floor level.

At the same time that the Heurtley House was being built, Wright was supervising the construction of what many consider to be the first masterpiece of the Prairie Houses: the Ward W. Willits House in Highland Park, Illinois, from 1901. The Willits House presents a formal, almost symmetrical, facade to the street and established the precedent for Prairie Houses with symmetrical wings. The long, low-roofed *porte-cochère* at the front entrance balances the low-roofed porch at the end of the dining

room. Inside, the ground-floor rooms—living, dining, pantry, and kitchen—pinwheel off the massive central chimney. Behind the kitchen are a flight of service stairs, two servants' bedrooms, and a bathroom. On the second floor, off a narrow corridor, are three fitted bedrooms, two further bathrooms, a large nursery, and a linen room. The main staircase rises through the double height space: on the landing is a library, while on the floor below is a small reception room.

Once building commenced, Wright continued to refine and improve the designs for a house: seeing the spaces develop in three dimensions often gave him additional

ideas. The Willits House is evidence of this practice: in construction photographs, the second floor west wall of the south wing is all on one plane, but the house as it exists today shows that this wall was relocated about three feet further west. If left as originally planned, the stair hall would have been unextraordinary but the enlargement makes it an impressive space. Entering via the low (6ft 6in) entrance, the space dramatically opens up to a two-story chamber topped by an art-glass ceiling light and a statue of the Victory of Samothrace. This scheme must have pleased Wright, since he was to use it again in the Susan Lawrence Dana House.

As in all of his finest houses, the Willits House contains many fine details: the jewel-like art glass, the furniture, the wooden screens that divide the space between rooms and encourage passage from one space to the other, and, of course, the massive fireplace, the physical and spiritual center of the home. While Wright's carefully designed and furnished interiors are strikingly beautiful, homage must be paid to the

craftsmen who carried out the work. Chief among them were the Milwaukee cabinet maker and decorator George Niedecken, on whom Wright relied throughout the entire Oak Park period for the construction of the fixtures that went into each custom-built Prairie House, and Orlando Giannini of the company of Giannini and Hilgart, who was responsible for the art glass of many of the leaded windows, ceiling lights, and glass interior doors.

The Dana House—also known as the Lawrence House after Mrs. Susan Lawrence Dana's family—was to be Wright's most extravagant commission to date. Completed in 1904 after a two-year building program, initially Mrs. Dana wanted the old family Victorian mansion to be remodeled and enlarged in an Italianate style. As the design and building process progressed, however, remnants of the old house gradually diminished. The Lawrences had been a pioneer family in central Illinois and by the 20th century had become sufficiently established in society in Springfield. Mrs. Dana now want-

ABOVE: ARTHUR HEURTLEY HOUSE (1902), Oak Park, Illinois. The Heurtley House uses a pinwheel plan; its roof is almost identical to that of the Winslow House and the front entrance is reached through a Romanesque arch similar to the ones employed in the Dana and Thomas Houses.

ABOVE LEFT: FRANK WRIGHT THOMAS HOUSE (1901), Oak Park, Illinois. The first of his Prairie style houses to be built in Oak Park, Wright worked on it with Webster Tomlinson, the only partner he ever had. Nicknamed the "Harem," it was commissioned by James C. Rogers for his daughter and son-in-law and is renowned for its art glass.

ed a house that was both the family home and a tribute to the family—past, present, and future. Her wealth matched only by her eccentricity, Mrs. Dana, at the same time as being a suffragette and a philanthropist, kept in touch via a spirit guide with her deceased father, whose guidance was sought on all practical and financial matters.

The Dana House is a series of grand rooms: a two-story high dining room, a library, and an art gallery housed in a detached building linked by a pergola to the long arm of the T-shaped plan of the main house. The rooms were designed to accommodate social gatherings of several hundred of Mrs. Dana's closest friends, and for those

53

who tired of the highbrow talk at her parties, they could make use of the built-in bowling alley in the basement.

The original Lawrence house stood on a plot that was several feet higher than the level of Fourth Street, which it faced. The new Lawrence-Dana House, with its broad, low-modeled gables flashed with copper, maintained the elevated position but had a new entrance cut from Lawrence Street, named naturally enough after one of Springfield's most prominent families. The visitor approaches the entrance via a flight of low steps, through two Romanesque archways and under a vaulted space filled with art glass depicting stylized wild flowers common to the Midwest of America—sumac, purple aster, and goldenrod—which harmonize with the overall palette of the house. Outside, buff-colored Roman bricks are set off by a band of bronze luster tiles. Inside, oak furniture is combined with brown and russet fabrics. In addition to the decorative accessories, the furniture, fixtures, fittings, and textiles were all made to Wright's design specifications.

Halfway between the basement and the first floor—part of the house is designed using the raised basement principle—is the entrance landing. On this stands a terracotta obelisk, designed by Wright and executed by Richard Bock, called "Flower in the Crannied Wall," after a line in a poem by Tennyson. As the obelisk tapers to its apex, it is transformed into the figure of an idealized female nude, who is placing the finishing touches to the finials of a skyscraper.

At the landing, visitors are offered the option of descending the main staircase to a bathroom and a long passage leading to the library, or ascending to the salon, the dining room, living room, the late Mr. Lawrence's (Mrs. Dana's father) study (which was retained from the old house and incorporated into the new and where, no doubt, his spirit felt at home), the late Mrs. Lawrence's (Mrs. Dana's mother who died shortly after the house was completed) bedroom, and the art gallery. Mrs. Dana's husband, who had died only a few months before her father, does not, however, have a dedicated room.

A second impressive flight of stairs leads to the happy widow's bedroom, two guest rooms, two servants' rooms, several bathrooms and to a narrow balcony which overlooks the vaulted, two-story high dining

ABOVE: THE SUSAN LAWRENCE DANA HOUSE (1902–04), Springfield, Illinois. A 35-room mansion, the Dana House is the largest and finest example of Wright's Prairie House style to survive. A magnificent integration of architecture, interiors, and furnishings, the project took two years to complete and involved a painstaking eye for detail.

RIGHT: THE LAWRENCE MEMORIAL LIBRARY (1905). In addition to her own home, Susan Lawrence Dana commissioned Wright to design a small library as a memorial to her father, who had died in 1902. The commission was unusual in that it required Wright to design an interior space within an existing building, an elementary school.

room. Outside, behind a two-story wood and masonry screen, was the garden and a reflecting pool.

The contrast between the Heurtley House—while smaller, it is no less a jewel—and the Dana House demonstrates the adaptability of the Prairie House formula. Wright's solutions could be simple or complex, one or two storys, made of masonry or a light frame structure, be faced in stucco, brick, stone, or shingle. Finally, the Prairie House was equally at home in the neat city suburbs with their carefully manicured lawns or in the middle of a forest or on the edge of the Great Lakes.

Falling within the Prairie House formula was the group of buildings which Wright designed from 1902 for his Aunts Nell

and Jane Lloyd Jones for the Hillside Home School. The original school buildings designed by Joseph Lyman Silsbee—possibly with assistance from Wright—had now been outgrown and the aunts turned to their nephew with the commission for his first major construction on family land; it would turn out to be the precursor for his own home at Taliesin North.

Hillside Home School II was constructed out of local sandstone with special attention paid to the site and to the surrounding landscape. The school buildings utilize the Prairie House horizontality, which is enhanced by the chimneys and the slotted windows. The main feature however is not Prairie House, but a series a of tall, cross-shaped pavilions with two-story tall bays; these house a gymnasium, an assembly hall, a drawing studio, and a science laboratory. The west (gymnasium) pavilion is linked to the east (assembly hall) pavilion by means of a gallery flanked on the south side by classrooms, below which are the manual training

THE SUSAN LAWRENCE DANA HOUSE (1902–04), Springfield, Illinois.

LEFT: The interiors of the Lawrence Dana House demonstrates the total integration of architecture, furnishings, and decorative arts. More than 450 pieces of art glass and over 100 pieces of oak furniture were designed and produced by Wright and his studio over two years.

ABOVE: The motifs in the magnificent art-glass windows of the Lawrence Dana House are based on butterflies and the sumac, a native tree of North America.

RIGHT: One of more than 200 lighting fixtures designed by Wright for the Lawrence Dana House.

FAR RIGHT: Designed by Wright and executed by Richard Bock, the sculpture "Flower in the Crannied Wall" stands at the entrance landing of the Lawrence Dana House.

areas. The northern axis of the school is a bridge link between the assembly hall and the two other pavilions which are disposed in a T-shape.

The following year Wright designed a narrow three-story Prairie House in Oak Park for W.E. Martin, the president of the Martin and Martin Stove Polish Company of Chicago, which manufactured the E-Z brand of stove polish. While the W.E. Martin House is often regarded as being one of Wright's least successful houses—the site is really too small to do justice to the Prairie House formula—the significance of the commission cannot be underestimated since it marked the beginning of Wright's involvement with

the Martin family that would eventually lead to the commission for the Larkin Building.

William Martin's brother Darwin lived in Buffalo, New York. Visiting his brother in Chicago, he was so impressed by the new house that he also commissioned Frank Lloyd Wright to design and build two houses on his land in a new development in Jewitt Parkway, Buffalo.

Darwin's principal business was the Larkin Company, a mail order and wholesale firm which specialized in soaps and household staples. The senior management of the company not only had a common interest in the success of the business but were related to each other through marriage. The co-

founders were John Larkin and Elbert Hubbard: Hubbard's sister married John Larkin; a second sister married the company's chief attorney, W.R. Heath. The Heaths and the Martins were close friends and when Hubbard retired from the Larkin Company in the 1890s to move to East Aurora, some 30 miles southeast of Buffalo, to establish the Arts and Crafts community of Roycroft, Darwin D. Martin took over his position and brought Alexander Davidson into the company as advertising manager. Wright's connection with the Martin brothers and their business interests would eventually lead to nine building commissions: the William E. Martin House at Oak Park; the Darwin D.

LEFT: THE GEORGE AND DELTA BARTON HOUSE (1903), Buffalo, New York. Commissioned by Darwin D. Martin for his sister and brother-in-law, the two-story main block contains the reception area, living room, and dining room on the first floor and four bedrooms on the second.

BELOW: THE WILLIAM E. MARTIN HOUSE (1903), Oak Park, Illinois. This is a three-story house of plaster and wood-trim at 636 North East Avenue. The building was restored to a single family house in 1945 after many years of being split into three apartments. Originally landscaped by Burley Griffin, little of his work now remains.

RIGHT: THE WILLIAM E. MARTIN HOUSE (1903), Oak Park, Illinois. For Wright, the hearth was the "sacred heart" of a building since it signified the idea of family life.

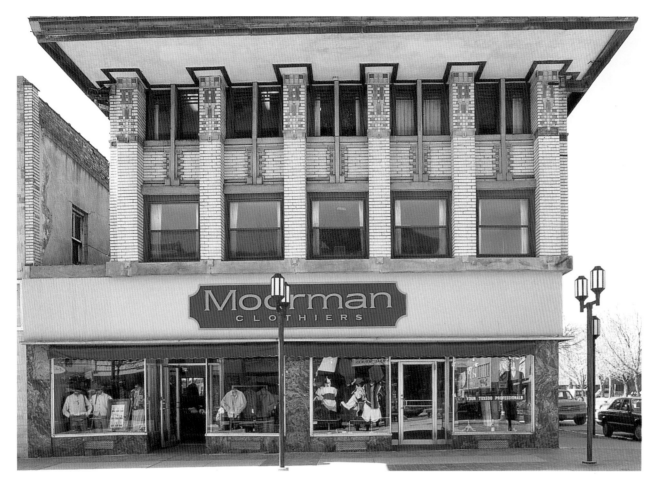

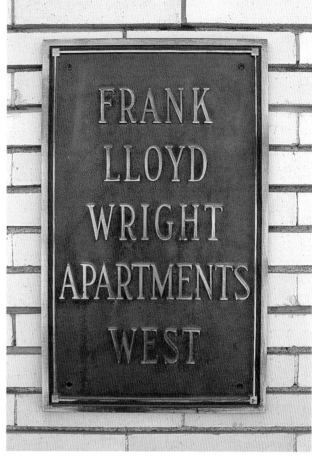

Martin House; the W.R. Heath House; the Barton House; the Alexander Davidson House (all in Buffalo); the summer residence for Darwin D. Martin at Derby, New York; the Larkin Building; the E-Z Polish Factory in Chicago and an exposition building for the Jamestown Tercentennial of 1907.

Darwin D. Martin proposed building two houses on a large flat area of land he owned in Jewitt Parkway: one house was to be his own home and consists of the main house, a garage, and a conservatory. The second house was to be the home for his sister and brother-in-law, the George Bartons. Although commissioned by Martin, this house has always been known as the Barton House.

The smaller Barton House—built of the same warm red Roman brick as the Martin House—was the first of the pair to be built and reduces the Prairie House formula to a strict symmetrical plan. This house, with its side entrance on Summit Street, along with the communal greenhouse and garage—Mr. Martin favored the automobile

over horses—is set at the rear of the main or Martin House, which fronts onto the Parkway running parallel to the buildings behind it. The main house is joined to the Barton House by a long pergola. As well as unifying the plan, the pergola also provides protected access to the greenhouse and divides the gardens from the kitchen yards. Contained in the pergola's basement area are steam pipes used for heating the two homes, while the furnace is housed in the garage. The rectilinear greenhouse is the site for a marble replica of Wright's favorite classical sculpture, the Victory of Samothrace, which is visible from the front door of the Martin House over 100 yards away!

The main part of the Martin House is a low, two-story block: on the left is the *porte-cochère*, on the right a covered porch. Bisecting the house is the entrance hall and to its right is a large room, divided by partitions. The central space functions as the living room and has a huge, wide fireplace. The two flanking spaces serve as the dining room and a library. These two rooms are light-

filled spaces because of the long rows of windows, but the living room is darker as it is in the shadow of the roof of the porch. As an afterthought, Wright cut a skylight through the floor of the bedroom gallery directly above the living room to increase the amount of light. To the left of the hall is a second living room, Martin's private office, toilets, and the kitchen.

The house is heated by banks of shoulder-height radiators housed in perforated oak cupboards and the space between the top of the cupboards and the ceilings are filled with small leaded casement windows which open into the adjoining rooms. As in the Dana-Lawrence House, Wright was given an unrestricted budget in the Darwin D. Martin House, and with it he created one of the most complete Prairie House interiors: light fixtures, rugs, hangings, furniture, and even the grand piano were all designed by Wright, with the wood for both the furniture and the trim of the house a honey-colored oak. Once again, the glass is the handiwork of Giannini, who also provided the glass

tesserae for the chimneybreast mosaic, which incorporates a Japanese style wisteria motif and was designed by Blanche Ostertag, who also designed the similar mosaic overmantle in the Husser House.

The E-Z Polish Factory, which Wright designed for the Martin brothers in 1905, was significant for a number of reasons: after nearly a year's continuous absence from Chicago working on the Buffalo projects, Wright's return was to be marked by a new interest in non-domestic projects—factories, retail shops (the Pebbles and Balch Shop, Browne's Bookstore, and the Thurber Art Gallery) and office interiors like the redesign of the entrance lobby of the Rookery Building. Like the Roloson Houses, the E-Z Factory was a lost Wright building until 1939, when it was rediscovered by G.C. Manson who spotted it from the window of a train! More importantly, the E-Z Factory marked Wright's first use of reinforced concrete and in the building he would perfect the methods to be used in the construction of Unity Temple.

At the beginning of June 1904, the wooden frame church of the Unitarian congregation in Oak Park burnt down. Although Wright had been a member of the congregation for many years, the fact that the pastor, Dr. Johonnot, awarded him the commission was surprising since Johonnot was not considered progressive in his taste: his vision for the new church was for a New England style meeting house with a tall spire. What he got was a concrete structure with a cantilever roof! Original Wright plans specified a building in brick and stone but it appears that the potential offered by concrete—the medium he was using in the E-Z Factory at the same time—was irresistible. Furthermore, congregation funds for the new building were restricted and therefore fine masonry and other materials were simply beyond the budget. For $35,000 Wright had to provide a church with an auditorium and parish house for a congregation that numbered well over 400 people. Out of the funds also had to come the cost of materials and the cost of labor. One of the main causes of the delays

in the construction of the building was the simple fact that the workers employed on the project were not familiar with the techniques of building in this new material and many wholeheartedly disapproved of its use outside of factory buildings.

The exterior of the church is a monolithic mass of concrete. The walls, with their rough surface, were left undressed, exactly as they emerged from the wooden moulds into which the concrete was poured and in which it dried. Over time, the surfaces have

weathered down to a golden hue and in parts vines and creepers have grown, softening the building's appearance. The impression that the viewer receives—inside and out—is that they are looking at an arrangement of Froebel's kindergarten "Gifts"—building blocks arranged on top of and next to each other. The plan of the cube containing the auditorium is a Greek cross inscribed in a square and the space inside it is filled with different levels of seating. Over the center of the cross, the ceiling reaches its high-

ABOVE: THE HOYT HOUSE (1906), Geneva, Illinois. While it is still a Prairie House, the Hoyt House demonstrates the versatility of Wright's scheme: it has a square plan and scaled down decoration to meet the restrictions of Hoyt's limited budget.

RIGHT: THE STEPHEN M.B. HUNT HOUSE (1907), LaGrange, Illinois. One of Wright's "budget" Prairie Houses, as with the Hoyt House it has scaled-down decoration and has been reduced to the most basic architectural form—a cube.

est point and is almost completely formed out of a skylight. The four short arms of the cross have slightly lower ceilings and have banks of windows at the top. Placed between the arms of the cross are stair towers whose roofs are lower still.

Unity Church not only marked a definite break with traditional ecclesiastical architecture but it was a pioneer American building in reinforced concrete. Only in France, in the architecture of Auguste Perret and Tony Garnier and by a mere four years, had its use been anticipated.

The largest non-domestic commission which Wright undertook between the completion of the Unity Church and the building of the Midway Gardens complex in 1913 was the City National Bank and Hotel in Mason City, Iowa. This was begun in 1909 and the project was sponsored by the law firm of Blythe, Markley, Rule, and Smith. Mr. Markley's daughters were pupils at the Hillside Home School and an accidental meeting between Wright and Markley at the Lloyd-Jones's resulted in the commission.

The law firm wanted a structure that would function as a civic center in which were the facilities of a bank, a hotel (to be known as the Park Inn and to be Wright's first venture in hotel design), and retail shops. In the plan of the building, Wright allowed the various functions of the elements to dictate the layout, resulting in an asymmetric composition of buildings which spread along a long axis. The two main areas, the bank with business offices above it and the hotel-cum-shopping building, are linked together by the lines of the heavily projecting roof slab.

Among Wright's other non-domestic commissions during this period were two clubhouses. The River Forest Tennis Club of 1906 is in the Prairie House formula: a long axis that terminates at each end in diamond-shaped bays and a strongly horizontal elevation with no vertical accents other than three squat chimneys. It is a design which in many ways anticipates that of the Robie House. On the other hand, the commission for the Fox River Country Club, which stood midway between Batavia and Geneva, Illinois, was

the brainchild of an eccentric millionaire, Colonel Fabyan. Fabyan's estate already by 1906 consisted of a number of buildings and outbuildings, including a genuine Dutch windmill that he had shipped over and re-erected as a sort of landmark.

Fabyan's ideas for the development of his estate were elaborate and for some time Wright was involved in the scheme. Nevertheless, only one project was to come to fruition—the remodeling by Wright of a large old building on the estate to serve as an exclusive, private recreational center for a select number of families who lived in the Fox River valley. The resulting building, which was destroyed by fire a few years after completion and never rebuilt, was largely dictated by the existing structure of the old building and, unlike the Prairie House which was soon to reach its full flowering, this building harked back to an earlier phase in Wright's œuvre. Widely spaced French doors and tapering chimneys gave the building an unusual verticality. Wright also made a start on the remodeling of Fabyan's own house

TOP LEFT: ISABEL ROBERTS HOUSE (1908), River Forest, Illinois. A medium-priced Prairie House, the site allowed for a more horizontal treatment than was usual.

TOP: THE HOYT HOUSE (1906), Geneva, Illinois. While it shares many of the features of the largest Prairie Houses—the overhanging eaves and the raised ground floor level—the square plan of the Hoyt House is rare in Wright's buildings of this period.

ABOVE: RIVER FOREST TENNIS CLUB (1906), River Forest, Illinois. The clubhouse was one of Wright's few non-domestic commissions from the Prairie House period.

RIGHT: UNITY CHURCH (1904), Oak Park, Illinois. Today known as Unity Temple, Wright called it "my little jewel box"; its interior is rich with art glass and fine wood trim.

ABOVE LEFT, ABOVE, AND RIGHT: THE EDWIN H. AND MAMAH BORTHWICK CHENEY HOUSE (1903), Oak Park, Illinois. The main living areas rest on a raised basement (which housed Mrs. Cheney's sister) and stretch the entire length of the front of the house, while to the rear are the bedrooms. The wood trim of the walls and ceiling were stained dark red according to Wright's specifications. At the center of the plan for the Cheney House Wright situated the living room which opens onto the dining room (Right).

but, before any significant work took place, Fabyan and Wright ended the project by mutual agreement.

The years between 1905 and 1910 were the heyday of the Prairie House. In that time nearly two thirds—some 40 houses— were designed. Some were planned for limited budgets, using mass-production techniques and with the usual Wrightian decoration scaled down to reduce costs. Examples of this type of Prairie House include the Sutton House (McCook, Nebraska, 1907); the Hunt House (La Grange, Illinois, 1907); the Adams House (Highland Park, Illinois, 1905); the Fuller House (Glencoe, Illinois, 1906), and the Hoyt House (Geneva, Illinois, 1906).

The Hunt and Hoyt Houses are examples of the Prairie House reduced to its most economic form for popular housing: the simple cube. The square plan, however, remained the exception in Wright's work until later on. At this time, he never used it if the budget permitted an alternative scheme. The windows of these small houses were sometimes leaded in simple geometric pat-

terns; more often than not, they were subdivided by wooden mullions into the more conventional squares and diamonds. Where budgets permitted, Wright sometimes included "Tiffany Bricks"—a term used between 1890 and around 1910 to describe light brown Roman bricks with small, dark, vitreous marks and holes caused by silicon fuzing during firing. Because of their antique mottled color, the bricks resemble the glass produced by Louis Comfort Tiffany. These bricks were often used for facing the chimneys in the living rooms of Wright's low budget houses.

The medium-priced Prairie Houses included the Isabel Roberts House (River Forest, 1908), the Alexander Davidson House (Buffalo, 1908), the Steffens House (Chicago, 1909), and the unbuilt Guthrie House (Sewanee, Tennessee, 1908). This price bracket allowed for a more horizontal treatment and was capable of enlargement and while some were two storys tall, others were bungalows. The blending of Prairie House principles with the bungalow was something

with which Wright first experimented in the design of the house for Edwin and Mamah Cheney in Oak Park in 1904.

Finally, there are the two outstanding Prairie Houses, whose size or quality place them in a class all by themselves: the Avery Coonley House (Riverside, Illinois, 1908) and the Robie House (5757 South Woodlawn, Chicago, 1906).

The Coonley house was the product of a rare mix of a progressive and enlightened client with an unlimited budget and belief in the ability of their chosen architect. According to Wright's biography, the Coonleys had examined every project that he had built to that date before contacting him. Seeing this as a compliment, Wright stated that he put his best work into the Coonley House. The house was perfectly suited to its site: Riverside was laid out in 1869 by

Frederick Law Olmsted at the instigation of the Chicago, Burlington, and Quincy Railroad as a model suburb. The perfectly flat land was cut by an irregular, winding street plan. The Coonley House was planned for a roughly triangular plot at the edge of the Olmsted plan and was nearly surrounded by the meanders of the Desplaines River. The nature of the terrain is mirrored in the meandering plan of the house—the main house, the garages, and out-buildings also seem to meander across the landscape.

In the long, U-shaped plan of the house, two of Wright's strongest beliefs were put into practice: the centrifugal plan and the raised basement. All the main rooms of the house—except for the large centrally located children's playroom—are located on the second level above ground height and every room that is devoted to enjoyment looks out over lawns and the garden from a carefully calculated height. The outer walls have a banded effect: the lower parts are coated in a creamy-colored fine sand plaster, while the

ABOVE: THE CHENEY HOUSE (1903), Oak Park, Illinois. The fireplace not only provides the central hearth and heart of Wright's homes: here the masonry backs onto a long gallery which effectively divides the house into two with bedrooms at the rear of the building and public rooms at the front.

RIGHT: Another view of the Cheney House living room. Raised above street level the main living areas extend the entire length of the house; for added privacy, the leaded casement windows are raised above the eye level of passers-by on the street outside.

upper parts are faced with bronze-colored tiles with a geometric surface pattern. The most frequently published view of the

Coonley House is of the front garden with its terraces, huge, shallow Wrightian planters, and the beautiful reflecting pool.

Inside, the Coonley House is zoned within the U-shaped plan: the living and dining rooms together with the service areas are located in the western half of the U while the bedrooms are located in the eastern half. In order that both the family or communal rooms and the master bedrooms should look out onto the gardens to the south, the central bar of the U is divided between living and sleeping quarters. Inside, a harmony of shapes and textures has been created by the furniture and fittings, all of which were designed by Wright. The color scheme is in Wright's preferred autumnal hues: natural oak, browns, russets with touches of gold, and greens, all enriched by the light which falls through the leaded casements and ceiling lights. Because of its sheer size and its custom-built furnishings, the Coonley House

was a long-term project and even after completion a major alteration was made. It was decided that gaining access directly to the outside from the playroom—the space directly beneath the living room—was too difficult and a row of French doors opening onto the reflecting pool were installed in the place where originally there had been three low windows under a continuous lintel. In 1911, a second major addition was made in the shape of the Avery Coonley Playhouse, a small building built in the grounds designed to serve as a playhouse and gathering place for neighborhood children.

While the Coonley House setting was largely rural—almost literally in a Midwestern prairie landscape—the Robie House was Wright's consummate Prairie House adapted to an urban site (although when it was erected, Chicago's South Side was still a somewhat leafier suburb than today). Frederick C. Robie was a successful bicycle manufacturer,

engineer, and amateur automobile designer. According to Robie he had sketched his idea for a house and showed it to a few builders who told him that what he wanted was really one of "those damn Wright houses." The house which Wright designed for Robie satisfied both client and architect, and fully integrated the elements of design that had been developed in the earlier Prairie Houses. In the Robie House Wright eliminated the basements and set the building on a concrete base. Brick piers and steel beams provided the structural framework upon which the three tiers of the house rest. The landmark, low-hipped roof with its wide projecting eaves—20-foot wide cantilevered terrace roofs—continues to impress viewers. The overall horizontality of the house is reinforced by the narrow bricks with raked mortar joints. With no room for a garden, Wright ingeniously landscaped nature into the massive planters and urns and at each level,

ABOVE LEFT AND ABOVE: THE AVERY COONLEY HOUSE (1908), Riverside, Illinois. One of the most outstanding examples of the Prairie House, the Coonley House was the product of a rare mix of outstanding architect and enlightened clients with an unlimited budget. In this house Wright put into practice two of his strongest beliefs: the centrifugal plan and the raised basement. In this way all the main rooms are located on the second level above ground height and every room devoted to enjoyment overlooks lawns and gardens.

LEFT: The Coonley House is a harmony of shapes and textures. Fixtures and fittings—all designed by Wright— conform to a color scheme of autumnal hues of natural oak, browns, russets, and touches of gold.

doors and windows open onto terraces, balconies, and porches extending the interiors outside and bringing nature inside.

The Robie House is arranged along a single axis, running parallel to the long dimension of the corner lot it inhabits. Integral to the building—perhaps for the first time in American architecture—is the garage. Wright, like Robie, shared a fascination for automobiles and this may explain why the

ABOVE: THE HEATH HOUSE (1905), Buffalo, New York. Although smaller in scale than the great Darwin D. Martin House, in the Heath House Wright also employed the same massing of brick masonry, the facing with red Roman bricks, and russet tiles.

RIGHT: THE ROBIE HOUSE (1906), Chicago, Illinois. This is the Prairie House par excellence. Designed in its entirety, the Robie House is enriched inside with furnishings, art glass, and lighting fixtures that demonstrate all the earlier design elements of the Prairie residences fully integrated into one of the most imposing buildings of the 20th century.

garage accommodates not one but three cars, has an engine pit, and a car wash!

Nicknamed "The Battleship"—no doubt because many saw the three levels as "decks" and the projecting terraces as "prows," the entrance to the Robie House is hidden on the north side of the building. Inside areas which demand privacy—guest bedrooms, kitchen, servants' rooms—are located in a parallel block at the rear of the main block. The living room, central staircase, and the dining room create a single unit, separated but not divided by the chimney. The master bedrooms are contained in the smaller area of the third level of the house, a sort of glazed loggia topped by the low umbrella-like roof.

Wright, once again, designed the Robie House in its entirety: the interiors rich with furnishings, light fixtures, rugs, and magnificent art glass. The house, including

the land on which it stands, cost Robie the princely sum of $59,000. But just two years later in 1911, the client who Wright described as a man with "unspoiled instincts and untainted ideals" was forced to sell when both his marriage and his business failed. In 1957, the Robie House faced demolition but was saved by a property company who later transferred ownership to the University of Chicago. Now the Robie House is a National Historic Landmark and one of 17 structures designed by Wright to have earned special recognition from the American Institute of Architects as representative of his contribution to American culture.

It is a pity that a third magnificent Prairie House project ended in failure, since the proposed McCormick House of 1907 intended for Lake Forest, Illinois, would surely have outranked both the Coonley and Robie Houses in magnificence. The largest

house ever designed by Wright, it was commissioned by Harold McCormick, the heir to the famous reaper and farm equipment designer's fortune. McCormick had apparently been interested in a building by Wright for some time and in 1907 proposed that Wright should draw up new ideas for the McCormick family home at Lake Forest (about 30 miles north of Chicago). The site selected for the new house was indeed dramatic: a large piece of land bordering the bluffs which rise from the beaches of Lake

Michigan. There was also the added feature of a natural brook cascading through a deep ravine at the southern edge of the property. In a favorable atmosphere, Wright proceeded to design a huge complex of main house and ancillary buildings, to be located on the natural bluffs which had been reinforced by means of a series of retaining walls. The height of the walls was to vary so that no single horizontal axis became dominant. On top of the platform provided by the retaining walls—some 50 feet up—the long composition of the house with its associated pavilions and galleries would range.

If the plan had gone ahead, the McCormick project would not only have placed Wright at the forefront of avant garde architecture, it would also have put the seal of approval on the whole progressive movement in architecture in America and most likely stemmed the still flowing tide of eclecticism and historicism. The story of the rejection of Wright's design has never fully been revealed. It was suggested that Mrs. McCormick was the driving force behind its rejection on the grounds that her mode of life was not suited to living in a Prairie House. Not surprisingly, a woman who had married into a family whose fortune was reputed to be as large (if not larger) than the Carnegies' and the Morgans', preferred instead to commission a handsome, though far less innovative, Italian style villa by the master of traditional architecture, Charles Augustus Platt (1861–1933).

RIGHT: TALIESIN (1911, REBUILT 1914 AND 1925), Spring Green, Wisconsin. On land originally owned by his mother's family, Wright began designing buildings for members of his family as early as 1887 with Hillside Home School (pictured) for his aunts Jane and Nell. In 1902 part of the school was redesigned and in 1932 it was remodeled to accommodate the Taliesin Fellowship. In 1895 he designed and built the Romeo and Juliet Windmill to provide water for the home and school and in 1907 designed "Tanyderi" for his sister Jane and her husband Andrew Porter. In 1911 Wright returned to Spring Green to build a new home and new life for himself and Mrs. Cheney. Following a family custom he gave his home a Welsh name—"Taliesin" meaning "shining brow."

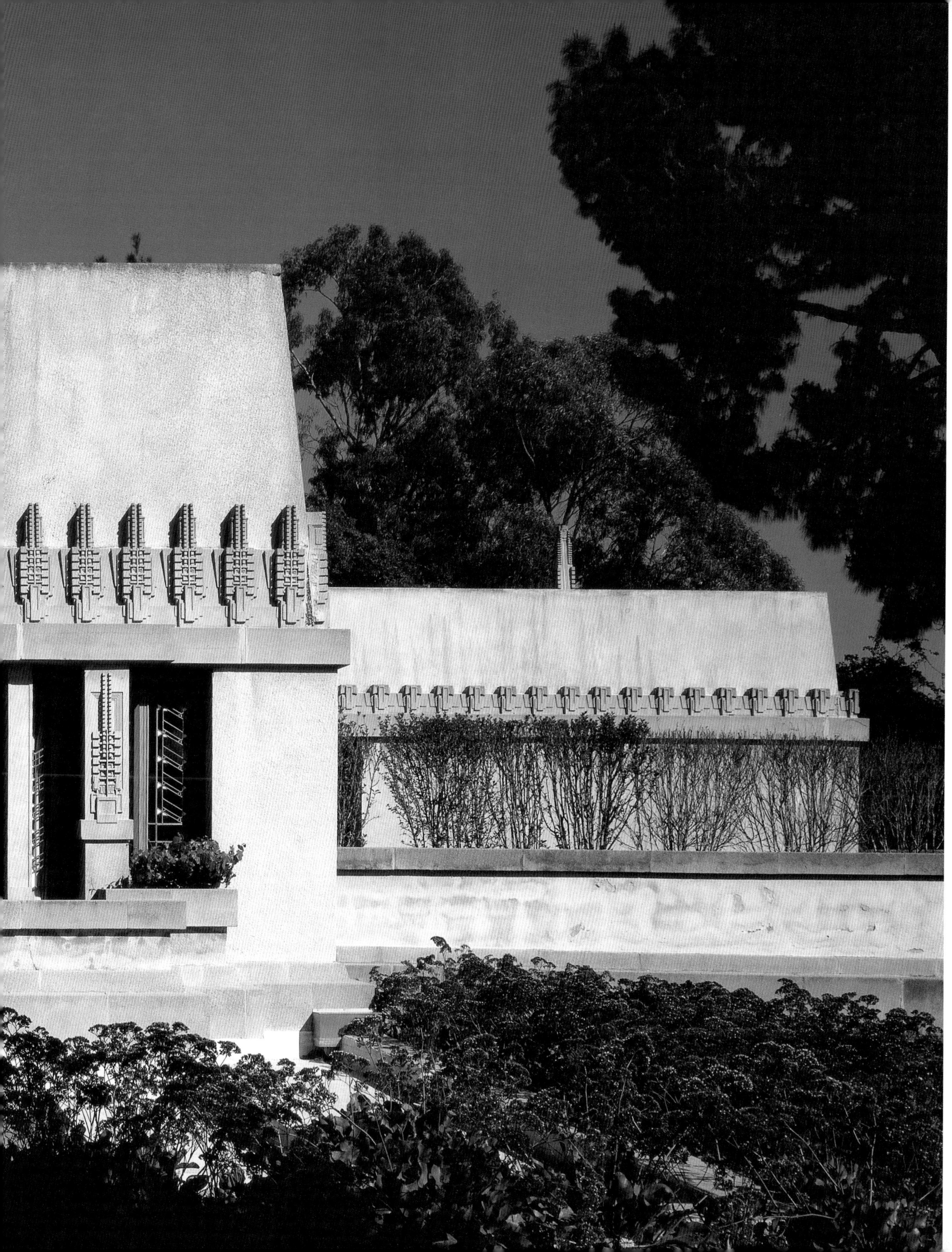

A NEW PLACE, A NEW MEDIUM

A NEW PLACE, A NEW MEDIUM

The E-Z Polish Factory, built for the Martin brothers on Chicago's West Side in 1905, was Wright's earliest experiment in the use of reinforced concrete, although as early as 1900 he had envisaged its use in the plan for "A Village Bank," published in *Brickbuilder* magazine in 1901. By the time of the E-Z Factory, few buildings in America had been constructed in reinforced concrete. "Poured stone," as it was called, was more often considered a poor substitute for traditional masonry, and most structures, including the new developments in skyscrapers, were heavily adorned with U.S.-inspired decorative facades and ornamentation which hid the underlying steel and concrete structures.

In the 1920s Wright began to focus his attention on developing a standardized system of concrete block construction, and between 1922 and 1932 he worked on at least 30 projects, five of which were to be realized. According to Wright's autobiography, the idea of building with concrete blocks formed gradually after he had returned from Japan in 1921; he had been living and working there for five years on the Imperial Hotel project in Tokyo. With the hotel complete, further hopes for major commissions in Japan failed to materialize and Wright returned to the United States. Immediately on his return, Wright went to Taliesin and remained for five months.

The exact reason for Wright's relocation to California is not known; in his autobiography he sheds little light on the event. It is likely that a number of factors led to the move: he had been ill with dysentery in

ABOVE AND PREVIOUS PAGE: THE ALINE BARNSDALL HOUSE (1911–21), Los Angeles, California. Better known as the "Hollyhock House," the large and expensive complex for Aline Barnsdall got its nickname from the stylized flower motif that is used on the exterior frieze and interior ornamentation.

Tokyo and was physically exhausted; he was still married to Catherine and his relationship with Miriam Noel was under increasing strain. Consequently, the opportunity to relocate to a sunny climate and a state where large tracts of land for building were available at very low prices may have appeared to Wright as offering a "new beginning"—professionally and personally.

Furthermore, earlier in 1909 Wright had already built one house on the West Coast. The design for the George C. Stewart

House at Montecito, Santa Barbara was completed in the Oak Park Studio a few months before Wright's notorious flight to Europe with his mistress Mamah Borthwick Cheney. Because of his sudden departure, the construction of the Stewart House went unsupervised and numerous changes were made to Wright's original plans—the service wing was enlarged, the attached garage was reworked into a kitchen and the open second floor sleeping balconies were glassed in. Nevertheless Wright included a perspective drawing of the house in the Wasmuth portfolio published in Berlin in 1910—the avowed purpose of his trip to Europe.

Since 1920 Wright had also maintained an office in Los Angeles which was staffed by his son Lloyd Wright and Rudolph Schindler (1887–1953). Schindler had been born in Vienna and trained in architecture and engineering under Otto Wagner at the Vienna Academy of Fine Arts. In common with Wright, Schindler had come under the influence of one of the leading theorists of modern architecture—Wagner, like Wright's mentor Louis Sullivan, was a considerable force in writing and building at the turn of the century. Schindler also had contact with the work of architects Josef Hoffmann, Josef Olbrich, and Adolf Loos, who was the author of *Ornament and Crime* (1908), a famous essay on architecture.

As a result of what he saw in the 1910 Wasmuth portfolio of Frank Lloyd Wright's designs, Schindler became keenly aware of Wright's contribution to new architecture. He decided to go to America partly out of his

Taliesin, Wright met Aline Barnsdall in Chicago. An heiress to millions and a self-proclaimed "new woman," Barnsdall had taken over the running of a small theater in the city. A woman convinced that she could change the world—albeit according to her own beliefs—Barnsdall found Chicago somewhat less receptive to her theatrical ideas than she had hoped. Seeking a new audience for her works, she purchased a 36-acre plot of land in East Hollywood, Los Angeles and commissioned Wright to design the house that was to be named after her favorite flower. It was to sit at the top of "Olive Hill" (Barnsdall also named the hill!) and look out over olive and citrus groves to the Pacific. On the slopes of the hill Barnsdall planned for a theater and a number of smaller buildings to be used as rehearsal and dance studios as well as apartments and retail units to serve a Los Angeles community of avant-garde artists.

Although Wright knew that the Imperial Hotel project would mean extended absences from America and that Ms.

interest in Wright's work but also because of America's technological supremacy. On his arrival in Chicago in summer 1914, Schindler secured a job in the firm of Henry A. Ottenheimer, Stern, and Reichart. Although he had intended returning to Europe, the outbreak of World War I made it difficult and Schindler eventually settled in California, where he began working for Wright in 1917. It was to be a tense relationship, due in part to Wright's frequent absences in Japan and also to his profound belief in his abilities as an architect of genius. Wright became convinced that Schindler was usurping his place as designer on many of his projects. In fact, Schindler was doing what Wright himself had done during his employment at Sullivan and Adler's firm in Chicago—Schindler had started his own independent architectural practice and from his office in the Schindler

ABOVE AND RIGHT: Details of the Aline Barnsdall House. The plan of the house encloses a large garden court which terminates in what was originally a circular reflecting pool (ABOVE). The stylized hollyhock motif (RIGHT) is repeated on stucco pinnacles on the exterior, the art-glass windows, and in the carved backs of the dining-room chairs.

Chase House on King's Road, Hollywood (a two-family house built in 1921 for himself and his friend, the engineer Clyde Chase) he designed buildings which display inventiveness and flexibility.

To a large extent, Lloyd Wright and Schindler were responsible for overseeing the realization of Wright's second—and probably most recognized—California design. The Aline Barnsdall House, better known as the "Hollyhock House," was begun in 1917 and continued until 1921—years which, for the most part, Wright spent in Tokyo.

Shortly after Mamah Borthwick Cheney's death in the fire that engulfed

Barnsdall was a difficult client who would be unlikely to settle with dealing with his project supervisor—even if it were his own son—Wright, nevertheless, accepted the commission.

The "Hollyhock House," a large and expensive complex, appears at first sight to be a monolithic concrete building. In fact, its structure is composed not of concrete but of hollow clay tiles covered with stucco. The block-like simplicity is relieved only by the use of abstract patterns in the form of the stylized hollyhock motif.

The main public rooms of the "Hollyhock House"—entrance loggia, living room, music room, and library—are organized in a T-shape, a device Wright had used frequently in many Midwestern Prairie Houses of the early 20th century. The "Hollyhock House," however, has two extended wings housing bedrooms and nursery in one, kitchen, dining room, and servants' rooms in the other. The living room is dominated by the central fireplace with a decorative overmantle and projecting hearth surrounded by a pool of water. The large sculptural forms of the seating group—also designed by Wright—create an intimate space within the larger space of the room. Barnsdall's desire for a building that was half house and half garden, was provided for in the numerous terraces, colonnades, and pergolas that link the interior spaces with the exterior spaces of the gardens. The two wings enclose a garden court and, as in the Robie House, entry to the "Hollyhock House" is complex: one enters from the side through the long, entry loggia.

The "Hollyhock House," two guest houses, and a spring house were the only structures completed in the lengthy building program. A fourth structure, known as the "Little Dipper"—a projected Community Playhouse—was begun but never completed. The "Little Dipper" was intended as a private school for Barnsdall's daughter Betty, but it was also to be open to local children who would pay for their tuition. In its aims the "Little Dipper" recalls the Avery Coonley Playhouse, built 12 years earlier for the Coonleys who also wanted to give their only daughter a progressive education in aesthetic surroundings.

Barnsdall's peripatetic lifestyle—on a mere whim she would take off on a voyage to some distant place—and her annoyance and disappointment at a house too large and at a cost too great eventually resulted in her abandoning the main residence in favor of one of the smaller Wright-designed buildings on the site. In 1924 Barnsdall turned to Rudolph Schindler to transform the incomplete "Little Dipper" into a garden seating area, pergola, and pond. Schindler used Wright's reinforced concrete block construction to complete the project, but severe damage in the 1994 earthquake led to partial demolition that means only the retaining walls remain.

It is true to say that in the "Hollyhock House," Wright was "guilty" of the same "sin" for which he frequently condemned his contemporaries: the lack of honesty in the use of materials and structure! Nevertheless, it is also true to say that the "Hollyhock House" also illustrates Wright's long-term interest in primitive, non-European forms—particularly pre-Columbian architecture. Along with the Ho-o-den reconstruction at the World's Fair, Wright would also undoubtedly have seen the reconstruction of the Mayan Nunnery at Uxmal. Wright's interest in Mayan architectural forms and in the decorative use of Mayan-inspired cast-concrete, first manifested itself in the small warehouse built for Albert Dell German (pronounced "Jarman") in Richland Center in 1917.

German was a wholesale commodities dealer who planned to expand his business, and commissioned Wright to design a new warehouse. Wright conceived a four-story structure, whose brick walls rise from the concrete base and are crowned by an intricate frieze in contrasting gray concrete. Incorporated into the geometric design of the frieze are 54 windows. The reinforced concrete structure is designed with a grid of massive concrete columns reinforced with steel and with flaring capitals which carry the weight of the floor and the roof. On the capitals of six of the columns, the motif of the external frieze is repeated. The double brick-wall skin of the building created a cold storage without the use of mechanical refrigeration while eliminating the interior wall allowed for maximum internal storage space. In addition to providing storage for German's wholesale goods, the structure was also to contain a restaurant, retail shopping units, an art gallery to display the works of regional artists, and space dedicated to the display of Wright's own handiwork.

How Wright came to be offered this commission is something of a mystery, although local legend has it that Wright owed German a substantial sum of money for supplies he had purchased over the years and had never paid for—Wright volunteered the design of the new warehouse as a way of discharging the debt. By 1919, the estimated construction costs, which had started out at $30,000, had reached $125,000! In 1921 German was forced to halt the construction work: scaffolding was removed and the entrances bricked up. While many in Richland Center must have struggled to have found beauty in the rather lump-like cube that stood out in strong contrast to every other building in their town, recent commentators have remarked on the similarity of the warehouse's shape and appearance to the Mayan Temple of the Three Lintels in Chichen Itza in Yucatan.

Like so many of Wright's clients, German continued to have a strong faith in Wright—despite all the troubles and anxieties that accompanied working with him—and in the 1930s he asked Wright to remodel the now derelict interior. Financing proved impossible and German eventually lost the building through bankruptcy proceedings;

subsequent owners leased the building for storage and light manufacturing industries. Today, the warehouse is still unfinished but renovation in the 1980s provided a gift shop and a small theater on the ground floor, while there is an exhibition space dedicated to Wright's work on the second floor.

Shortly after his arrival in Los Angeles Wright began further experiments with concrete blocks but at this stage he was mainly concerned with the massing and ornamental aspects of the building and not really with their structural system. It was in the enormous project for oil millionaire Edward H. Doheny that Wright first envisaged the use of the concrete textile blocks.

In southern California Wright hoped to devise an altogether new style of architecture, a key aspect of which would be the use of inexpensive concrete blocks which were easy to manufacture, required only unskilled labor to erect, and were easy to maintain without exterior paints or protective coatings. In Wright's hands, these concrete blocks could in themselves provide interesting shapes and decorative patterned surfaces, and he spoke of this system as providing reasonably low cost housing to millions of Americans across the country.

For some time Wright had been trying to develop a concrete wall slab and to this end he and his son Lloyd Wright had been working on methods to link blocks together with steel rods that extended vertically and horizontally from one block to the next to create a wall of any length and height. Two sets of linked blocks created the exterior and interior walls. Between the two walls was a hollow space, which allowed air to circulate, keeping the structure free of damp and the building cool in summer and warm in winter. The steel rods ran through channels along the tops and sides of the blocks and, once fastened together, were sealed in place with concrete grouting. The result was a thin, but strong, reinforced slab wall. Because the wall could be made of blocks which were molded with a repeated pattern, Wright described himself as a "weaver" of what he called "textile" blocks.

To judge by Wright's plans, the Doheny Ranch project, where numerous concrete-block houses were to be built on the terraced hillsides of the Santa Monica Mountains above Beverly Hills and linked together by roadways, tunnels, and bridges of the same construction, would have been one of Wright's most important and large-scale ventures, and one where many of the problems in design and construction of the concrete-block system would have been resolved.

The client always associated with the project was Edward Lawrence Doheny (1856–1935), who had struck oil near Los Angeles in 1892 and within a few years had established the city as a major player in the oil industry. Doheny's reputation, however, was severely tarnished by his involvement in the Teapot Dome oil-leasing scandal of 1922—although he was later exonerated of anything more than bad judgement. Doheny owned a 411-acre site made up of nine separate parcels of land which were acquired in 1912 and developed as a working ranch and weekend retreat for his family.

In the end, nothing came of Wright's plans and many speculate that the proposals and designs were little more than a dream. Certainly there are inconsistencies: Wright always referred to the client as Edward *H.* Doheny and the site as being to the east of Los Angeles in the San Gabriel Mountains. It is possible that the scheme was simply a joint venture between Wright and real estate developer John B. Van Winkle for promotional purposes, since no site plan has ever been found.

Indication of the block system appears in rough sketches on drawings for two further houses in early 1923: one of the houses was for Aline Barnsdall, who was already contemplating quitting the

LEFT: THE ALICE MILLARD HOUSE (1923), Pasadena, California. "La Miniatura" was Wright's first realized concrete textile-block house in California.

"Hollyhock House," the other was for the famous "La Miniatura," the Alice Millard House. The sketches show two blocks formed to interlock with a hollow space between them and expanded metal is indicated for the assembly system. However, in the finished drawings for these two houses, the system is not worked out in any greater detail and it was only with the restoration of the Millard House and the opening of the walls that it became possible to see Wright's method of assembly in detail and discover that he had started from a concept different to the well-publicized one that followed.

There are two types of basic block: each is 15½ inches square and they are assembled in pairs. The patterned blocks were used primarily for the exterior walls, and plain blocks used only in the interiors. Each block is designed to interlock: the patterned blocks have flanged edges that connect with semicircular cavities in the plain blocks. The blocks in the Millard House have no reinforcing metal rods but are laid with expanded metal on a conventional mortar bed; the second house—designed for Aline Barnsdall for a site in Beverly Hills—followed the same pattern, but, as with so many projects for this client, it was never built.

"La Miniatura," built from 1923 in Pasadena for Alice (Mrs. George Madison) Millard was Wright's first concrete-block design to be constructed. Seventeen years earlier, Wright had designed a house for the Millards in Highland Park, Illinois. Mr. Millard had been one of the country's best known dealers in rare books. Now a widow, Mrs. Millard had continued her husband's business combined with her own—buying and selling antique European furniture. Millard wanted a small, romantic house that would serve both as a home and a shop, but she had a limited budget.

Eager to try out his new system of construction, Wright described his textile blocks to Mrs. Millard and pointed out that they would provide a fireproof building for her husband's valuable collection of texts. Furthermore, the limited budget was not a problem for Wright, who, anxious to try the system, offered to design the new house without charging his standard fee although he reserved an interest in the house in the form of a lien. He and Mrs. Millard signed a contract stipulating that Wright would be compensated in the event that the Millard House was sold speculatively for profit.

Mrs. Millard had already purchased a treeless plot in Pasadena but nearby she and Wright discovered a ravine in which stood two eucalyptus trees. What Wright and his client called a ravine was in fact an arroyo: dry for much of the year, in rainy seasons arroyos carry vast quantities of floodwater. Because of the amount and speed of flow of water through these arroyos, they are much more dangerous to live by than the more harmless ravines of the Midwest. Flying in the face of wisdom, Wright decided to build the Millard residence at the bottom of the arroyo. Having sold her original plot of land, Mrs. Millard was able to purchase the new arroyo land at an unsurprisingly cheap price!

Partly because the narrowness of the arroyo precluded the long, ground-hugging horizontality of the Prairie House style and partly because Wright's textile-block design favored the design of houses as multiples of cubes, the Millard House is a box. The north side of the house is placed next to a small lane; the visitor enters through a paved court leading to an entrance covered by a low bridge which spans from the house to the roof terrace over the attached garage. Inside, the two-story living room has a high window wall composed of glass doors at the lower level, and a pattern of perforated concrete blocks set with glass above. The square blocks, of which the house is constructed, are patterned with a central, sunken cross which is reminiscent of the pre-Columbian architecture of Mitla, near Oaxaca in southern Mexico. Wright originally designed a studio addition to the southwest of the main

house; this was carried out in 1926 by his son, Lloyd, who also doubled the size of the garage to hold two cars.

Like many of Wright's clients, Mrs Millard was delighted with the design of the house and it was only during construction that troubles began. The Pasadena building constructor A.C. Parlee agreed to build the house for $9,810 and the plans were agreed in March 1923 with work to be complete by October 1. There is no doubt that the experimental nature of the block system caused delays. Although in concept the construction was simple, more than one type of block was required—perforated patterned blocks, half blocks, quarter blocks, corner blocks, and the 8 inch by 16 inch rectangular blocks that are stacked in single vertical rows to frame the windows and doors and to form the piers at the entrance. Wright insisted that sand from the actual site be used for his concrete mix, his argument being that the color and texture of the concrete would be indigenous to the site. However logical this "organic" approach was, it nonetheless had many drawbacks; since it was impossible to remove the impurities from the local sand, the blocks proved to be unstable over time. Furthermore, the wooden molds for the blocks were to be made on site by Parlee's carpenter. One of these molds survives today and, despite age and weathering, it is apparent that they were not precision-made— because wood expands with moisture, the blocks produced from them were never uniform in size.

In January 1924, with work on the Millard House half finished, Parlee resigned from the project. In June he filed suit against Mrs. Millard claiming more than $12,000 compensation for additional work he said he had carried out because changes had been made to the original plans—Parlee claimed that the construction plans originally called for a single rather than double-block wall construction. Mrs. Millard testified that this had never been so and Parlee lost his case.

Rather than see his first experiment in the textile-block system left unfinished, Wright himself contributed $6,000 to its construction costs and the house was eventually completed in March 1924.

The lawsuit was not to be the end of Mrs. Millard's troubles, however: the decision to site the house at the foot of the arroyo would prove to be a mistake. Wright tells in his autobiography how the culvert, which had taken the street water away below the basement level of the house for 50 years, now overflowed and rose to the level of the dining room, burying the floors under layers of mud. The house was cleaned up with the help of the Pasadena City authorities, but Wright had still to sort out the problem of the leaking roof.

Several months after "La Miniatura" was started, Wright altered the method of concrete-block construction: henceforth the blocks were held together by a network of internal joints filled with concrete grouting and steel reinforcing rods. By eliminating the mortar joints, Wright could do away with skilled labor, while the addition of steel increased the structural and formal capabilities of the blocks—concrete works by compression but by adding steel reinforcement it gains in tensile strength. Around the same time Wright began the process of securing a patent on his new invention which encouraged new and untried applications of the concrete blocks.

The house for John Storer on Hollywood Boulevard was the second of Wright's Los Angeles textured concrete-block houses. Storer (1868–1933) was a homeopathic doctor from Chicago who had moved to California in 1917. Although always referred to as Dr. Storer, he had in fact failed the California medical licensing examination in 1919, and had turned instead to real estate development.

Parallel rows of hollow concrete-block piers on the front and rear elevations and paired piers on the end elevations support wooden beams and joists in the central volume of the building. The structural nature of the piers at the south end of the building is expressed by narrow, vertical windows which pierce the curtain walls. The central, high living room is a rectangular space set back from its surrounding terraces. The wings to each side—bedrooms to the west, service areas to the east—help enhance the dominant verticality of the central area. For the construction of the actual concrete blocks, Wright specified sand or decomposed granite. A formula of four parts aggregate to one part Portland cement was to be mixed in a mechanical mixer until it would stand up when squeezed by hand. Unlike the blocks in the Millard House, the Storer House blocks were to be formed under pressure in machine-made metal molds, which were more precise. The blocks were then removed from the molds and allowed to dry over a period of 10 days. Four different block patterns were used: the Storer House is the only building in which Wright used more than one design. There is a dominant pattern, however: one for the corner blocks which are decorated with a concave pattern of concentric half squares that read as a whole square when the two faces of the blocks are seen.

In charge of construction was Wright's son Lloyd, who was also the landscape architect and responsible for the illusion that the house was visible only in fragments—like the parts of an ancient ruin—in its jungle-like gardens. Although Dr. Storer moved into the house, shortly afterwards it was on the market and was sold in 1927.

The youngest and possibly least affluent of all of Wright's southern California

RIGHT: THE JOHN STORER HOUSE (1923–24), Hollywood, California. The second of Wright's concrete-block houses in the region, Wright hoped to develop an altogether new style of American architecture in which an important element would be the use of pre-cast concrete blocks which were cheap and easy to manufacture and did not require skilled labor to assemble. The concrete blocks themselves provided interesting shapes and decorative patterned surfaces; furthermore, as they could be subtly colored by the addition of local sand to the mixture, the need for traditional plastering and decorative paint finishing was avoided.

clients were the Freemans. Samuel was a jewelry salesman, Harriet was interested in modern dance: their building site was a small and steeply sloping plot in the Hollywood Hills. Its major feature was its view: below the site lay all of Hollywood. At approximately 120 feet, the Freeman House was the smallest of the block houses but also one of the most adventurous.

Responding to the needs of the Freemans and to the small site, Wright designed a concrete-block dwelling that was filled with light; it was airy and, in a manner not usually associated with concrete, very "delicate." The house was turned away from the street, opening it to the view: the front elevation is essentially a blank wall, while the back is almost entirely glazed. The plan is on two levels, with the living room and kitchen above, and two bedrooms and a bathroom below. Placed on the extreme boundary of the site, Wright took advantage of an extra wedge-shaped area of land to site the garage. Once again the contract between the Freemans and Wright stipulated the cost—$9,100—and a second agreement appointed Lloyd Wright as contractor. A final clause is reminiscent of the agreement with Alice Millard: if the Freeman House came in at a cost greater than $10,000, Wright agreed to finance the completion of the work and would be reimbursed if the property were subsequently sold.

Once again, as in the Millard House, problems in construction on the Freeman House soon appeared once building started. There was a problem with the land survey, and so Wright had to alter parts of his original design: in turn this forced up the costs of labor. Nevertheless, the Freeman House is one of the most beautiful of Wright's constructions. The abundant use of perforated blocks, often set with glass, and the breaking of the corners of the building with glass openings help suggest the intimacy of the interior. The metal mullions of the windows, which follow the pattern of the adjoining block walls, make the concrete walls appear more like thin screens rather than heavy masonry walls. The Freeman House also has the most adventurous of the block patterns: the house was designed to be constructed out of a single patterned block combined with plain blocks. There are both left-hand and right-hand versions of the square and chevron asymmetrically-patterned blocks, and sometimes they are turned upside down. Some commentators have described the pattern as an abstraction of the eucalyptus tree, although Wright never mentioned an organic interpretation.

The house incorporates the open plan and the central hearth of the earlier Prairie Houses and exploits the ornamental potential of concrete blocks combined with traces of Mayan, Mogul, Japanese, and European modernism. Wright never attempted to fully furnish any of his California block houses, although he did design some bookcases for Alice Millard. The Freemans turned instead to Rudolph Schindler for free-standing and built-in furniture, as well as for alterations to the building. The most significant changes occurred between 1928 and 1932. The wall between the west bedroom and the lounge was removed to create a larger space; the open loggia connecting the house with the storeroom under the garage was enclosed, and the storeroom itself converted into a small apartment.

The Freemans lived in their home for more than 50 years. At one point in what seems to have been a troubled marriage, the couple divorced, but because both of them were so fond of the building, both continued to live "separately together" in the house! On Mrs. Freeman's death in 1986, the house became the property of the University of Southern California, whose school of architecture is responsible for its maintenance.

The last of the concrete-block houses in southern California was built for Charles W. and Mabel Ennis and was the largest and most elaborate of all Wright's realized designs in this medium. Yet, in spite of the prominence of their house, little is known of the clients except that Charles and Mabel Ennis were the owners of a men's clothing store in Los Angeles: there is nothing to suggest why they became patrons of modern architecture and built an experimental house.

The site was on a steep mound at the base of the Santa Monica Mountains, elevated enough to be clearly visible from the city below. (Coincidentally, it could also be seen from Aline Barnsdall's house at Olive Hill.) The Ennis House occupies a site of approximately one and half acres, created by combining two adjoining lots; it is defined on three sides by Glendower Avenue. Wright's plan was for two buildings—the main house, and a chauffeur's apartment and garage—separated by a paved courtyard. Constructed of 16-inch square blocks joined by metal reinforcing rods, the Ennis House rises in stages from an enormous platform buttressed by a retaining wall. Unlike the compact and vertically oriented compositions of the Millard, Storer, and Freeman Houses, the Ennis House has a much more attenuated plan, with the principal rooms occupying the second level. The unifying element is on the north side of the house: the 100-foot long loggia which links the main rooms and sets them open to the views of the city below.

The division of the facade into zones of smooth and patterned blocks is continued on the interior walls, while geometric patterns in the art glass recall earlier designs in Prairie Houses. Once again a wisteria motif appears in the glass tile mosaic above the living room fireplace.

As was now a regular occurrence, construction was fraught with problems. The blocks were made from decomposed granite which had been dynamited from the site during excavations for the foundations. The aggregate was then passed over a screen of quarter-inch mesh and only the finer particles that fell through the screen were used for the blocks. By September 1924 Lloyd

Wright was wiring his father that the south walls of the house were bulging and cracking and the lower blocks popping! The Ennises were becoming increasingly alarmed and eventually assumed control of the construction, carrying out several modifications including adding several block courses to the lower walls and repositioning the front door. Inside the house, in addition to redesigned ceilings, a glass screen designed to separate the dining room from the loggia was not built, and the low wall separating the dining room from the living room was reduced by one full block course. Other changes included the addition of elaborate iron grillwork, a fireplace hood, chandeliers, and the replacing of the specified shale paving in the entry and loggia by gleaming white marble!

In 1940 the Ennis House was sold to radio personality John Nesbitt, who added a swimming pool and billiard room of Wright's design; however, the remodeled interiors and furnishings Nesbitt commissioned were never carried out as the "romance" between client and architect soon declined into all out war. The Ennis House continued to be bought and sold, its interiors still grand and ornate, and its southern wall bulging.

Nevertheless, for all their faults, the California concrete-block houses were to have functions beyond the domestic and many were to have starring roles in the movies: the Hammer Horror *House on Haunted Hill* used "real" exterior shots, and re-created in the studio, if not an "actual" house, at least the studio's idea of the interiors. In *Karate Kid II* viewers are treated to the sight of a functioning Frank Lloyd Wright bathroom; but for most Wright fans the concrete-block house was at its most perfect as Harrison Ford's home in Ridley Scott's *Bladerunner*.

While the Ennis House marked the end of the California concrete-block houses, it was not the end of Wright's visions for concrete-block construction: there were three further projects which, although generally less well known, were more ambitious. One of them, a resort for Emerald Bay at Lake Tahoe, was started early in June 1923 during

between 1907 and 1909, and in 1918 had spent six weeks with Wright at Taliesin. McArthur's father, Warren, was also familiar as one of Wright's early patrons. The precise extent of Wright's involvement in the design of the complex remains unclear: McArthur's signature appears on the drawings for the project and he was responsible for the over-

LEFT: THE ENNIS HOUSE. Joined together with metal reinforcing rods, 16-inch square concrete blocks, when cast in patterned molds, become both decorative and structural. When parts of the south wall began to bulge and crack, Charles Ennis assumed control of the construction of the house and he and his wife made several structural modifications. The swimming pool—designed by Wright—was added by the second owner, John Nesbitt, in the 1940s.

BELOW: The wisteria motif in the glass of the Ennis House is treated in a stylized manner, which recalls Wright's earlier designs for art glass in some of the Prairie Houses of the 1900s.

ABOVE RIGHT: THE ARIZONA BILTMORE HOTEL AND COTTAGE COMPLEX (1927), Phoenix, Arizona. The complex of buildings is recognized as the result of a collaboration between Wright and Albert Chase McArthur, a former draftsman in the Oak Park Studio.

Wright's brief sojourn in Los Angeles. The others, a residential compound in the remote Death Valley and a new fraternity house for the University of Wisconsin, are from a slightly later period. None of the projects were ever completed and it can only be assumed that the same structural system Wright had employed in the Storer, Freeman, and Ennis Houses would have been used.

Wright's first opportunity to exploit the system after leaving Los Angeles came in 1928—an invitation from Albert Chase McArthur, the architect of the new Arizona Biltmore Hotel in Phoenix. McArthur was interested in using Wright's concrete-block construction system and approached him for permission. Wright would be paid $10,000 for rights to use the system. He agreed and traveled to Phoenix in January. He worked closely with McArthur for five months, offering advice about a system with which he personally had very little experience since it was Lloyd Wright who had supervised the construction of the California houses. McArthur had worked in Wright's studio at Oak Park

all plan of the hotel and cottages. Yet, during Wright's five-month stay in Phoenix, the refinements of the plans made during this period were more likely his and he was paid an additional $1,000 for six drawings that depict the building essentially as completed.

The hotel complex occupies 200 acres of a proposed 621-acre development. In front, the entrance wing projects from the main four-story block which contains the lobby, dining room, and sun room on the first floor, with guest rooms on the upper levels. The magnificence of the lobby is enhanced by the second-floor balcony and a ceiling covered in gold leaf. The floor, laid in concrete and stained green, has an incised motif that corresponds to the dimensions of the unit blocks. The building is not, however, organized on the 16-inch module that Wright recommended, but instead on blocks that measure 18 inches by 13 1/2 inches: six blocks form one nine-foot unit, an innovation that appears to be entirely McArthur's idea. Throughout the hotel and cottages, patterned and plain blocks are combined as in

the California houses. But unlike the angular, abstract patterns that Wright had used, McArthur used blocks patterned with subtle curves in both perforated and solid versions. To the rear of the hotel, two wings extend and partially enclose a hexagonal patio: one of the wings houses the polygonal ballroom in which 10 great beams rise like the spokes of a great wheel to support the roof.

Once again construction continued slowly, as there were construction problems and delays as well as tensions between McArthur and Wright. But, surprisingly, the Arizona Biltmore Hotel opened on February 23, 1929, only a little behind in schedule and after only six months' construction. Banner headlines in the local papers praised the achievement of McArthur, who was credited as architect. Wright was mentioned in passing as consultant. Nevertheless, within months McArthur was trying to dispel rumors that Wright had, in fact, been the architect. In April 1930 McArthur finally asked Wright for a formal statement which clarified to all, the exact nature of the relationship vis à vis the

Biltmore. Two months later Wright replied, writing that "Albert McArthur is the architect of the building," a statement which McArthur felt compelled to publish in 1941 following the publication of two books which he felt mis-stated the facts.

A number of details within the building make it apparent that much of the Arizona Biltmore is indeed the work of McArthur. Furthermore, during its construction Wright was already busy with a new project, the plans for San Marcos in the Desert, a new resort hotel and complex that was the brainchild of Dr. Alexander Chandler, the founder of a new town 24 miles south of Phoenix.

San Marcos in the Desert was to have as little physical impact on the landscape as possible: excavation was to be minimal and the hotel would have been suspended above the sloping ground on cast concrete piers and supporting walls, which used the desert floor as their foundations.

When Wright first undertook the design, he proposed camping near the site and doing some experiments with the concrete. Also, since the bank was close to foreclosing on Taliesin, he needed more commissions and somewhere to work. In January 1929 Wright brought to a low mound rising from the desert about a mile south of the Salt Range, an entourage of 14 people including his wife Olgivanna and their two children, six draftsmen, Will Weston (a long-term carpenter and handyman at Taliesin), Weston's wife Anna who would be the camp's cook, two of the Weston children, and a Mrs. Daigle, a governess for Wright's children!

Though Wright had always wanted to camp in the region, he also confessed that it would be more economic for his party to construct their own accommodation rather than rent it. Ocatillo—Olgivanna had suggested this by mis-spelling the name of the native plant—Wright's home in the desert was "founded" and within a couple of months of it being finished, photographs were appearing in German and Dutch archi-

ABOVE AND RIGHT: THE ARIZONA BILTMORE HOTEL. Ten great beams support the roof of the polygonal ballroom which occupies one of the two wings. These wings extend at the rear of the hotel and partially enclose an hexagonal-shaped patio.

LEFT: The magnificent lobby with second-floor gallery and ceiling covered with gold leaf.

tectural magazines, and later in magazines throughout the world. Wright had intended Ocatillo to be a temporary structure and, indeed, within a year it had vanished. The Wrights had gone back to Taliesin for the summer and planned to return to the desert in winter; then, in October 1929, the Stock Market crashed and Dr. Chandler was forced to put off the building of his dream resort. While Wright remained in Taliesin, in Arizona local Indians were plundering the wood from Ocatillo for firewood. Shortly before he "broke camp," Wright had constructed a plaster mock-up structure from the blocks intended for San Marcos in the Desert and, because of the climate in Arizona, whole specimens survived at the site into the 1960s.

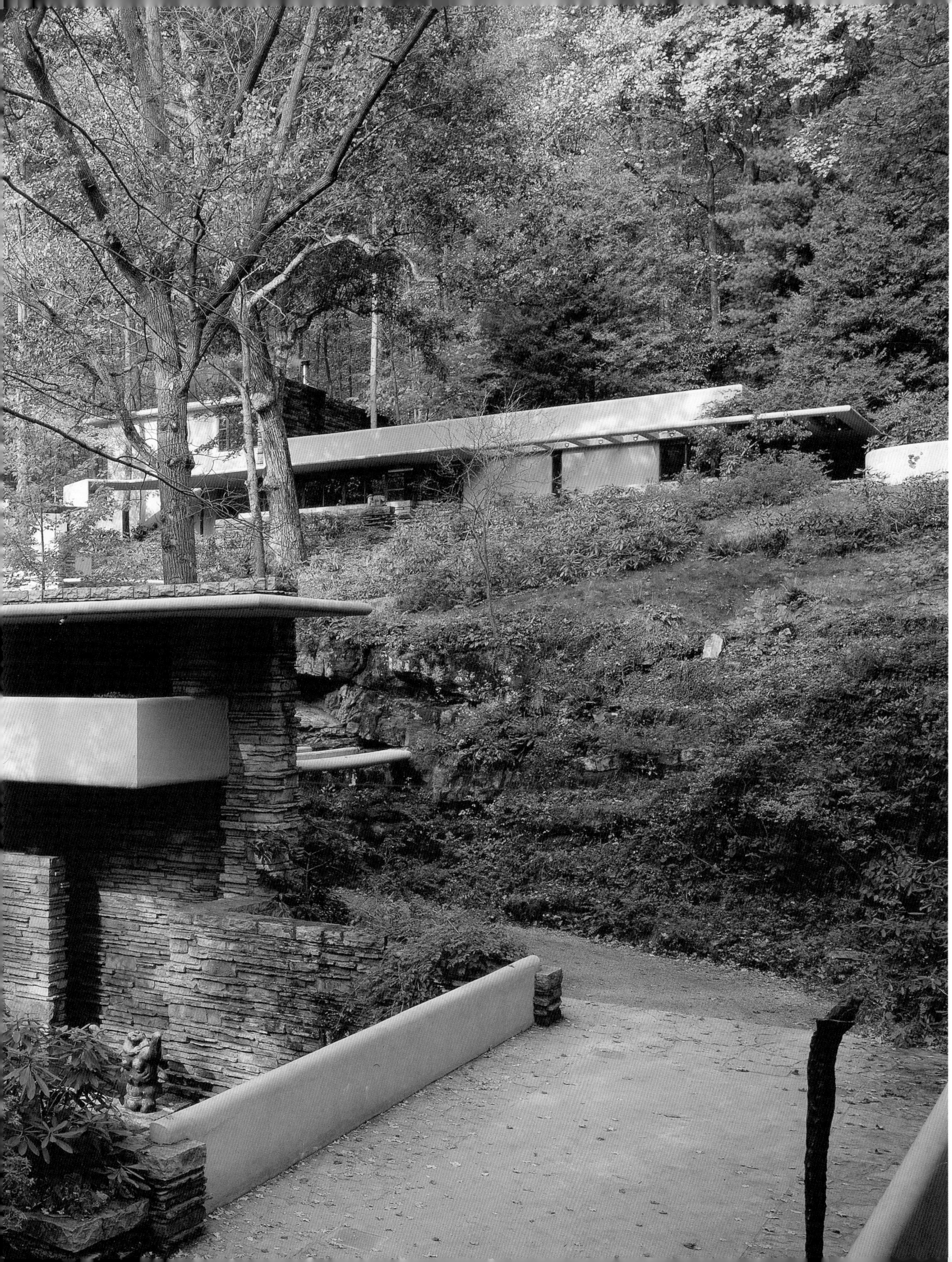

THE USONIAN HOUSE

THE USONIAN HOUSE

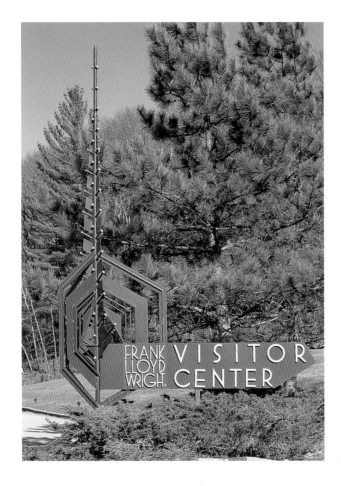

The 1930s were to be the years in which Wright produced some of his most accomplished works, including the Johnson Wax Administration Building and the famous house for Edgar Kaufmann—"Fallingwater." Yet one of Wright's most important contributions to architecture in these years was his solution to the problem of the small house with the development of the so-called "Usonian" house.

The 1930s also saw the establishment of the Taliesin Fellowship at Spring Green in Wisconsin in 1932. The Fellowship—really the brainchild of Wright's wife Olgivanna Hinzenberg, whom he married in 1928—was a means to extend the concept of organic architecture into a lifestyle. Students at the Fellowship worked in the gardens and fields producing their own food, did household chores, drafted plans, and constructed build-ings in order to create a complete approach to understanding architecture.

The Taliesin Fellowship was modeled on earlier "art colonies": Gurdjieff's Institute for the Harmonious Development of Man at Fontainbleau, France (Olgivanna had been a student there and Gurdjieff visited the Taliesin Fellowship in 1935); C.R. Ashbee's Guild of Handicrafts in Chipping Campden in Gloucestershire, England (Ashbee had been a frequent visitor to the United States and a guest at Wright's home in Oak Park); and Elbert Hubbard's Roycrofters in East Aurora, New York (Hubbard had been a founding partner in the Larkin Company).

Originally Wright envisaged some 70 "apprentice-fellows" and reserved the right to accept or reject any applicant at any time—even after they had been accepted into the Fellowship for, according to Wright, it was the apprentice who was on trial, not the Fellowship! Furthermore, in addition to four hours of physical labor each day, fellows also had to pay a fixed fee of $650 per year (the following year tuition fees were raised to $1,100 per year). It soon turned out that 70 fellows was a rather ambitious number and in the years of the Great Depression when such a large amount of money was hard to come by, it was not surprising that the number of fellows was lowered to 23—which exactly matched the number who actually commenced the Fellowship program on October 1, 1932. Hillside School, which Wright had remodeled in 1902 for his teacher-aunts Jane and Nell, was pressed into service now his aunts were dead: the class-rooms were converted into galleries, a dor-mitory was built to house the apprentices, and the gymnasium converted into a theater.

ABOVE LEFT AND FAR LEFT: The name Taliesin is now given to the whole complex of buildings at Spring Green, Wisconsin, although it initially related only to the main house. The Visitors' Center is housed in the former Riverview Terrace Restaurant, built in 1956.

ABOVE: TALIESIN (1911). Wright's summer headquarters, this part of the complex twice escaped destruction by fire.

PREVIOUS PAGE: THE EDGAR KAUFMANN HOUSE (1935), Bear Run, Pennsylvania. "Fallingwater" is probably Wright's best known work—in perfect harmony with its surroundings.

Today, the buildings continue to be used by the architectural school and by Taliesin Architects—the professional firm that is the successor to Wright's architecture and design firm. Additional space came with the construction of a 5,000-square foot drafting room as well as the long, low, red Midway Barns which were constructed to house livestock. In the 1940s a dairy (topped by a geometric spire) and a machine shed were added and in 1953 Wright designed what

today is the visitor's center as a restaurant: This project, however, remained unbuilt until 1967 and was constructed using steel trusses recovered from the flightdeck of the *Ranger*, a World War II aircraft carrier training ship!

Taliesin North, as the Spring Green "colony" was called, was to be Wright's summer headquarters: winters from 1937 onwards were spent at Taliesin West in Arizona. In 1937 Wright bought 600 acres of rugged and dry land—a pipe had to be driven 400 feet into the desert floor at Scottsdale in order to provide water—in the Sonoran Desert at the foot of the McDowell Mountains and established a second experimental "camp" that would serve as his winter home, studio, and "laboratory" of architectural ideas for the next 22 years. Over the years the complex was gradually altered and expanded to include a drafting room, offices

and studios, private living quarters, no fewer than three theaters, and a workshop, as well as accommodation for the fellows and staff.

Initially constructed of stone, cement, wood, and canvas, the structures seemed to grow naturally out of the desert as the textures and colors of the building materials blended with the landscape. As the buildings became more permanent, steel and fiberglass was used to replace the less durable materials. The living room at Taliesin West is dominated by the rugged masonry hearth and is framed by redwood forms that support the ceiling panels. The windows and hearth follow the triangular motif drawn from the shape of the surrounding mountains. The triangular shape is repeated in the "origami" armchairs which appear as though they have been folded out of wood. (A similar design of armchair appears in the in the John Storer

House [1923], and in the 1939 Sturges House "Skyeway.") At the heart of Taliesin West is the 96-foot by 36-foot drafting room, a communal dining room, and two apartments. Linking these "core" spaces is a terrace leading to the 56-foot long garden room with its sloping, translucent roof. Apprentices at Taliesin West live in apartments on site or in "tents" of their own design on surrounding land.

In addition to continuing the fellowship program established by Wright, Taliesin West is the international headquarters of the Frank Lloyd Wright Foundation, which owns and manages Taliesin at Spring Green, the Frank Lloyd Wright School of Architecture,

Taliesin Architects, and the Frank Lloyd Wright Archive, which contains 22,000 original drawings and nearly half a million other items related to Wright's life and works.

While the Taliesin Fellowship and the Frank Lloyd Wright Foundation today serve as testament to the achievement and continuing legacy of America's greatest architect, it is important to remember that, at the time of setting up the Fellowship in 1932, Wright was like many other architects in America: unemployed! Wright's last major commission had been a house for his cousin Richard Lloyd Jones in Tulsa, Oklahoma; this drew to a

close Wright's concrete-block experiments of the 1920s. It would not be until 1936 that commissions began to flow into the office once more.

Completed in August 1931, the flat-roofed Jones House was planned on a square grid; while it is only two storys high, it houses six bedrooms, a library, and billiard room, as well as the usual dining room, living room, kitchen, and servants quarters. Ornament in the Jones House is almost non-existent. Instead, identical concrete piers are alternated with panels of glass: the severity of the design gave the building a somewhat fortress-like appearance.

LEFT AND ABOVE: TALIESIN WEST (1937–59), Scottsdale, Arizona. In 1937 Wright established an experimental desert camp that would become his winter home, studio, and architectural laboratory until his death. The angled roofs, the exposed redwood beams, and the rubble and cement walls reflect the colors, textures, and forms of the surrounding Sonoran Desert at the foot of the McDowell Mountains. Constructed of stone and cement, the buildings seem to "grow" out of the landscape that inspired their design.

Despite the lack of commissions, several projects were on the drawing board at Taliesin: the fantastic scheme for the towers of St. Mark's in the Bowery, in New York City (This was a steel cathedral over 2,000 feet tall and the design would be the source, although on a much reduced scale, for the Beth Sholom synagogue in Philadelphia); the Elizabeth Noble Apartment House in Los Angeles; the continuation of designs for San Marcos in the Desert; and a plan for a complex of joined apartment towers in Chicago. Also on the drawing board were the plans for a "House on the Mesa," which was designed to be shown at an exhibition of contemporary architecture held at the Museum of Modern Art in New York in 1932. It was at this exhibition, organized by Henry Russell-

Hitchcock and Philip Johnson, that the term "International Style" was coined to describe the works of the European modernist architects such as Le Corbusier, Walter Gropius, and Ludwig Mies van der Rohe.

One project that was realized in the early years of the 1930s was the house for Malcolm Willey. Originally designed in 1932 as a two-story house, the Willey House was redesigned and built in 1934 as a single-story dwelling. The development of the designs for the Willey House marks a turning point in Wright's domestic architecture: the 1932 plans hark back to the Prairie House style, the 1934 version had the Willey House raised above the ground like the Robie and Coonley Houses, with the main living spaces on the second floor. The built 1934 version of the Willey House looks forward to the houses of the future, the Usonian Houses.

Between 1936 and 1941, when World War II virtually put a halt on all building except for military purposes, Usonian Houses sprang up all over the United States. The term Usonia is an acronym for the

"United States of North America": according to Wright the name came from Samuel Butler's novel *Erewhon*, although scholars have been unable to find the term used in that text. Whatever its origins, the idea of Usonia was Wright's key element in his response to the International Style of Le Corbusier and the like.

For Wright, Usonia was an idealized location for which he could design a wide variety of building types, ranging from homes and farm buildings, to gas stations, and civic centers; communities called Usonia I and Usonia II were planned for Lansing, Michigan and Pleasantville, New York. Only the last project was built—it was begun in 1947—and then only the first three houses were designed by Wright. It was expected that local architects would complete the scheme—subject, of course, to his approval—since by this time Wright was well past his 80th birthday.

The first Usonian House was for Herbert Jacobs in Madison, Wisconsin. Begun in 1936 and completed in 1938, the Jacobs House demonstrated Wright's com-

THIS PAGE: TALIESIN WEST. The forms and materials of the exteriors walls are also evident indoors where the masonry and exposed beams are both structural and decorative. The furniture, including the "origami" arm chairs of tropical hardwood, Douglas fir, and upholstered cushions are in keeping with Wright's ideas about Usonian homes and furnishings.

OPPOSITE: The entrance to Taliesin West.

plete rethinking of the small house. Herbert Jacobs, a journalist for the *Madison Capital Times*, and his wife Katherine had a small child and were by no means wealthy. They were, however, determined to have a house of distinction. At the time their ideal home was something in a Dutch Colonial style, but no such house was available in Madison. Katherine's cousin—who had spent some time at Taliesin—encourage the Jacobs to seek out Wright.

According to legend, the Jacobs were a little embarrassed by their poverty compared to the grandeur of their ambitions. Putting on a brave face at the meeting with the great architect, Mr. Jacobs jokingly stated that what America needed was a "decent $5,000 house." For 20 years, Wright said, he had been eager to design a low-cost house and here was his opportunity. Not only was Wright interested in low-cost housing, but the Jacobs House would serve as a small scale model for other commissions to be carried out on a larger scale.

Unfortunately, the Jacobs assumed that the amount mentioned included the cost of the building land! Wright let them find out the hard way and told them that until they had bought land he could not design. While Wright had urged for land in the countryside, the Jacobs opted for the suburbs and a plot of land that measured a mere 60 feet by 120 feet. It took up the $800 of their capital; the house itself would have to be financed by a mortgage. The poor Jacobses also believed that their house would be designed and built in three months: in the event it was well over

a year before they could move in, and even then the house was incomplete. To make matters more complicated, Wright encouraged the Jacobs to re-sell their plot back to the real estate agent who had sold it to them and to buy the two lots of land on the opposite side of the street—Wright was so confident that they would follow his instructions that he designed a house exactly 60 feet wide that would not legally fit onto the original plot of land! A further blow came when the Federal Housing Administration refused the Jacobs a mortgage because of the flat roof of

the design was against F.H.A. rules. In the end the Jacobs were "rescued" by a fan of Wright—a Madison banker who had enjoyed visiting Wright's Midway Gardens—who lent them $4,500 to build the house.

Instead of simply scaling down in size the traditional suburban house, Wright exploited the potential of the small size of the site by turning the back of the house onto the street and organizing the building around an L-shaped courtyard. Inside, the main innovation was to abolish the dining room as a separate enclosed space. In the Jacobs House, the kitchen is adjacent to the small dining area so that Mrs. Jacobs could watch over her children playing outdoors, talk with her guests, and prepare, cook, and serve a meal—all at the same time! The house gained almost instant public acclaim, largely because of its low cost at a time when America was emerging from the great depression and many young couples wanted the opportunity to become owners of a house in the $5,000 price range. Wright

called the Jacobs House *Usonia I* and like all "first examples" the house had several flaws: the steam circulation heating system proved inadequate and was eventually replaced with a hot water system; additionally, storm windows and screens were later added to "weather-proof" the house.

The next Usonian House was built for Paul R. Hanna, a Stanford University academic, and his young family. While generally considered Usonian, the eventual size and cost—which greatly exceeded the proposed budget of $15,000—of the Hanna House was beyond the means of most Americans at the time. Nevertheless, the grid plan, the interior and exterior walls of board-and-batten construction (designed so that they could be moved and rearranged—when the Hanna's three children were grown up, their section of the house was re-planned for new needs), and the central location of the kitchen workspace are characteristics shared by all of the Usonian Houses. In this house Wright abandoned the square or rectangle as the basic

unit for both the grid and plan in favor of the hexagon. This hexagonal schema gives the house its popular name: the "Honeycomb House." With walls joined at 120-degree angles, a fluid interior space and unrestricted views are created, further enhanced by the large amounts of glass that open out onto the brick terraces and the hillside.

The hexagonal module was used again in the Sidney Bazzet House in 1938 and, as in the Hanna House, brick is used in the lower sections of the walls while the upper portions and the roof are in laminated redwood. Over the bedroom wing the roof is low and horizontal; inside, the spaces are small and feel more like a ship's cabins. In contrast, the living/dining area, with its higher exposed gable roof, creates a more public space. The dining space projects out into one of the glass bays overlooking a terrace and, in common with many Usonian Houses of the period, there is a long built-in couch next to the fireplace, above which—pierced through the laminated wood—is a long row

of windows through which natural light penetrates. Tucked behind the brick fireplace mass is the small space of the kitchen.

Before the United States entered World War II, Wright had designed and built numerous examples of the Usonian House across America, from California to New Jersey, and after the war the concept remained equally popular. In 1943 Wright wrote that the moderately priced house was not only America's major architectural problem but also the most difficult problem facing its major architects. For most of his remaining career Wright was engaged in answering that problem, often through the Usonian House.

Another example is the Rosenbaum House in Alabama, a 1,540-square foot dwelling built at the cost of $12,000 in 1939. In an attempt to design and construct simpler, more efficient houses suited to the informality of American family life, Wright eliminated the basement and attic, embedding the heating pipes in the concrete floor

ABOVE LEFT: THE RICHARD LLOYD JONES HOUSE (1929), Tulsa, Oklahoma. The concrete-block experiments of the 1920s were drawn to a close with this house for Wright's cousin. Jones's four-acre plot overlooks the hills of the Arkansas River Valley and Turkey Mountain. Inside, patterned perforated blocks are used to house recessed light fixtures and to hide heating vents.

ABOVE AND BELOW: THE PAUL R. AND JEAN S. HANNA HOUSE (1936), Palo Alto, California. Based on an hexagonal, honeycomb module—accounting for its name of the "Honeycomb House"—the Hanna House appears more like an isolated country residence than the suburban house it really is, sited against a gently sloping hill; terraces provide additional outdoor living spaces.

slab and placing the mechanical systems and the plumbing near the kitchen-workspace. This approach, used in the Rosenbaum House, in many ways anticipated the prefabrication of many major building components: the walls, for example, were designed with an inner core of plywood that was sandwiched between board-and-batten interior and exterior surface walls. This did away with the need for traditional plaster and painted walls. Originally designed on an L-shaped plan on a two-foot by four-foot grid, the large living area included an asymmetrically placed hearth and dining area at one end, while at the other was a 100-foot long study area.

On the street side, the house appears as a nearly solid wall of Alabama clay and Southern cypress; reinforcing the overall horizontality of the building is the 20-foot long cantilevered carport. In contrast, the rear of the house has floor-to-ceiling windows, with doors opening onto the terrace and a Japanese garden, beyond which are woods.

Inside, fretwork wood panels frame clerestory windows and conceal the recessed lights. These are typical of Usonian Houses and articulate Wright's ideas about ornament being integral to the house. In his autobiography Wright set down the design features he considered essential to the Usonian House. These ideas ranged from that of a visible roof being expensive and unnecessary, to furniture, pictures, and bric-a-brac being unnecessary because the walls could be made to include them or even be them. In the Rosenbaum House the Wright-designed furnishings are supplemented by pieces designed by Charles Eames.

Two other outstanding examples of the Usonian House of this period include the Pope-Leighey House and the George D.

ABOVE: THE SIDNEY BAZETT HOUSE (1938-40), Hillsborough, California. The Bazett House continued the use of the hexagonal module, so successfully used in the Hanna House. The living/dining room space projects into one of the glass bays while the kitchen is tucked away behind the mass of the brick fireplace. The opening up of interior domestic space, which Wright had successfully introduced in the Prairie Houses of the 1900s, culminated in the Usonian Houses of the 1930s. Essential to the idea of the Usonian House was that furniture was largely unnecessary because the walls could be made to include it or even be it!—hence the long, low built-in settee and bookshelves are also part of the very structure of the house.

ABOVE RIGHT: THE EDGAR KAUFMANN HOUSE (1935), Bear Run, Pennsylvania. "Fallingwater"—Wright's masterpiece.

Sturges House, "Skyeway," which dramatically cantilevers over its hillside site in Brentwood Heights, Los Angeles. The solidity of the brickwork on the entrance side of the building contrasts with the sense of light-

ness of the deck, balustrade, and row of glass doors on the street side.

For Washington journalist Loren Pope and his wife, Wright designed a 1,200-square foot house for a cost of $7,000. Because of the design's radical nature, Pope could not get a mortgage (financing in the end came from his employer, *The Washington Evening Star*) and hired a builder who refused to sign a contract! Consistent with other Usonian designs, the Pope-Leighey House is modest in scale, has a flat roof with cantilevered carport, a heated concrete floor slab, recessed lighting, and uniform treatment of interior and exterior walls. The house was completed with plywood furniture built to Wright's specifications by Pope and the builder.

In 1963 the house was earmarked for demolition by the Virginia state highway commission. The house's second owner, Mrs. Robert Leighey, donated the building to the National Trust for Historic Preservation, who disassembled it and moved it 15 miles from its site in Falls Church to a similar wooded hilltop on the Woodlawn Plantation.

The cantilever feature of the Usonian House is nowhere better expressed than in Wright's most important and grand domestic commission of the 1930s, the house for Edgar J. and Liliane S. Kaufmann—"Fallingwater," the realization of Wright's romantic vision of man living in total harmony with nature. In 1934 Edgar J. Kaufmann Jr., partly as a result of reading Wright's autobiography, arrived at Taliesin. The son of a wealthy Pittsburgh department store owner, Kaufmann was to become an internationally famous historian and teacher. Visiting their son during his year long stay at Taliesin, the senior Kaufmanns fell under Wright's spell and within a few months they asked him to design a new planetarium for Pittsburgh (an unexecuted project), a new office suite for Kaufmann at the department store (which took two years to design and construct and is now housed in the Victoria and Albert Museum in London), and a country retreat for the Kaufmann family. Wright was also given funds to carry out work on the large model of his major project, Broadacre City.

Conceived first in theoretical terms after the stock market crash in 1929, Broadacre City was Wright's project for a new way of living. This theory, first published in full in 1932 in Wright's book *The Disappearing City*, took on a physical form during the Depression years through a three-dimensional 12-foot square model built in 1934-35: it was presented publicly along with

ABOVE: THE STANLEY AND MILDRED ROSENBAUM HOUSE
(1939), Florence, Alabama. A functional, cost-effective
Usonian House: at 1,540 square feet, it cost $12,000 to
construct. Basement and attics are eliminated, heating pipes
are embedded in the concrete floor mat and walls are a
plywood core sandwiched between board-and-batten interior
and exterior surfaces, which eliminate the need for
conventional plasterwork and decorative paint finishes.

BELOW RIGHT: The 20-foot long cantilevered car port
emphasizes the low horizontal profile of the Stanley and
Mildred Rosenbaum House.

FAR RIGHT: The Rosenbaum's large living room has an
asymmetrically placed fireplace with a dining alcove off to the
right. Fretwork plywood panels are used for both clerestory
windows and to conceal recessed light fixtures. The furniture,
designed by Wright, is complemented by pieces like the
dining-room chairs, by designer Charles Eames.

10 smaller collateral models at Rockefeller
Center on April 15, 1935. The Broadacre City
model described a four-square mile settlement to house 1,400 families and was organized by its transportation system and by
"zones of activity." Highways and feeder
roads were arranged to allow people to trav-
el to their work or leisure activities with the
minimum of inconvenience: Wright even
envisaged a hybrid vehicle which was part
automobile, part airplane: he called it an

"aerotor." In addition to small-scale manufacturing zones, the plans also accommodated
farming areas. A variety of housing types
were offered, and each family would have
one acre of land. "Cost saving houses,"
described as "prefabricated units," had glass
roofs and roof gardens.

The Kaufmanns owned a tract of land,
which included a stream called Bear Run, in
the mountains some 60 miles south of

Pittsburgh; although the family used to camp
on the site in summer, they now wanted a
year-round house. Wright visited the site,
noticed a large smooth boulder overhanging
a waterfall, and was told that Kaufmann liked
to sunbathe there and that the whole family
enjoyed swimming in the pools underneath
the falls. Wright told his clients that he wanted them to "live with the waterfall" as an
"integral part" of their lives and consequent-

ly built the house directly over the stream and anchored it with a series of reinforced concrete "trays" attached to the masonry wall and natural rock forming the rear of the house. These trays cantilever over the falls, appearing to float weightlessly above the valley floor.

For the novel structural engineering this project required, Wright depended on his right-hand man, Wes Peters, and a Chicago engineer, Mendel Glickman. Rather than move the large boulder on which Kaufmann sunbathed, Wright incorporated it into the design so that it served as the hearth. Wright also designed the Cherokee red circular cauldron that is suspended over the fire. The table-tops echo the cantilevered forms and three-legged chairs were designed to provide extra stability on the irregular stone floors. Sandstone quarried on site, concrete, and glass form the exterior and interior fabric of the building. The first-floor entry, the living room, and the dining room are integrated to form a continuous space. Dissolving the boundaries between interior and exterior space are walls of glass and wrap-round corner windows. A hatch opening to a suspended stairway allowed for ventilation and provided access to the stream below the house. The upper floors accommodate the bedrooms, which open onto private terraces.

As with Ocatillo, Wright's desert camp, "Fallingwater" became famous even before it was finished: throughout the world photographs appeared in newspaper and magazines, and a photographic portrait of Wright made the cover of *Time* magazine in 1938. Filling in the background was a drawing of "Fallingwater." But like all of Wright's commissions, the building of "Fallingwater" was not without its problems. Kaufmann had been somewhat surprised by the plans: he thought the building was to be located on the opposite side of Bear Run from which there was a splendid view of the waterfall. Wright in fact designed a house where it was actually impossible to see the waterfall!

Uneasy about having a house that hung in midair over a mountain stream, Kaufmann showed the plans to a Pittsburgh firm of engineers who advised against the scheme. When Kaufmann sent their report to Wright in Wisconsin, Wright in anger demanded that all work be stopped and that his plans be returned on the grounds that the Kaufmanns no longer "deserved" the house! Kaufmann apologized but it was not to be the end of their disputes. Kaufmann (acting on the advice of yet another firm of engineers) had the building contractor extend a stone wall by several feet to help support one of the cantilevered terraces. When Wright discovered this, he secretly ordered the top four inches of the extended wall to be removed, leaving the cantilever supported exactly as he had designed. When Kaufmann "confessed" to the change, Wright simply led him to the wall and pointed to the missing four inches: because the cantilever showed no signs of falling, Kaufmann agreed to the extended part of the wall being removed completely. Other disagreements included Wright's desire to cover the concrete

cantilevers in gold leaf and Kaufmann's wish to turn one of them into a swimming pool!

Along with the many Usonian Houses he was designing during this period and with the continued extensions and developments of the structures at Taliesin West, in 1938 Wright was working on the designs for the campus at Florida Southern University. The project was initiated by the president of the college from 1925 to 1957, Dr. Ludd Myrl Spivey (pronounced "spy-vee") an ordained Methodist minister and lifelong disciple of the philosopher John Dewey. Despite the fact that his college had little endowment, few wealthy alumni, a not very impressive academic record, and a student body (mostly of girls) who had to finance their own way through college through working, Spivey was determined that his college should prosper—particularly since it had managed to

ABOVE: THE LOREN POPE HOUSE (1940), Alexandria, Virginia. This house is now better known as the Pope-Leighey House after the second owner Mrs. Robert Leighey, who donated the building to the National Trust for Historic Preservation in 1963. The building had been designated for demolition by the state highway department so the National Trust dismantled and moved the building 15 miles to a new site on the Woodlawn Plantation.

BELOW RIGHT: The uniform treatment of the interior and exterior walls of the Pope-Leighey House are features of Usonian Houses, as are the clerestory panels, which also recall the leaded windows of the Prairie Houses. The clerestory panels allow wall space below to be used for built-in furniture and admit light from ceiling height. The interior is complete with plywood furniture that Washington journalist Loren Pope constructed to Wright's specifications.

weather the worst years of the Depression—and he envisaged a lakeside campus complete with chapel, library, administration building, faculty housing, student dormitories, classrooms, an industrial arts building, music, science and cosmography buildings as well as an art gallery with studio-workshop facilities!

Realizing that a building program was the best way of attracting attention, Spivey commenced fund raising activities for a new chapel—an appropriate building since the college's mission remained in part the training of Methodist ministers. Once Spivey had it in his mind to build there was no stopping him. Likewise, he had it in his head that Wright was the greatest American architect and that was just the credibility Florida Southern University needed—even though it appears that Spivey had no idea who Wright was and it was rumored that he had, in fact, confused him with a popular novelist called Henry Bell Wright!

In April 1938 Spivey wired Wright in Arizona requesting a conference to discuss his plans for, as he called it, "a great education temple." Spivey did not mention the fact that he didn't have any money to pay for this temple and, like many of Wright's clients, it came as a great surprise to him that the great architect agreed to undertake the design. Wright, as usual, was strapped for cash but was always optimistic that a fee would materialize! Yet, in this instance the lack of funds did not appear to worry Wright. Spivey was

offering him a major opportunity: to design the master plan for an entire campus, of which the hexagonal Annie Pfeiffer Chapel would be the centerpiece (and the main source of fund-raising). Wright agreed to lay out a plan that would eventually include 18 buildings—of which 10 were actually built.

Over the next 20 years, buildings of Wright's design took form. It was a slow process: Spivey would write to Wright complaining of the lateness in the delivery of plans; Wright would respond with apologies and promise their imminent delivery. Wright would complain to Spivey that he and his apprentices at Taliesin were in danger of starving to death if they did not get some money from him; Spivey would reply with apologies and nearly always enclose a check!

The tallest building of the complex—and the focal point of the plan—is the hexagonal Annie Pfeiffer Chapel, the strong vertical silhouette of which provides a visual counterpoint to the low, flat-roofed, rectangular seminar buildings built in 1940 and the circular reading room of the Roux Library built in 1945. Pierced blocks of the side walls of the chapel allow light into the auditorium

from the side, while from above light falls through the mass of slanting skylights supported by a skeletal steel tower.

The other Wright-designed buildings on the campus include the Watson Administration Building—actually two buildings separated by a courtyard containing a reflecting pool and connected by a walkway; the Orway Building, which has interior courtyards and houses the circular theater; the Danforth Chapel, and the three-story Polk County Science Building, which houses the only planetarium designed by Wright.

Once again Wright's ideas regarding "integrated ornament" are apparent in the contrast of smooth, textured, and perforated cast concrete blocks. Set into the blocks are abstract patterns of colored glass for decorative effect. Extending from the copper-trimmed roofs are trellises which Wright intended as supports for vines, and the garden "metaphor" is carried further in the large planters on the flat-roofed walkways and orange trees preserved from the original site on a hillside that falls away to a shallow lake.

One important aspect regarding Florida Southern University must not be

ABOVE LEFT: FLORIDA SOUTHERN UNIVERSITY (1938), Lakeland, Florida. On the site of a former orange grove, Wright set out to design the lakeside campus. Over the next 20 years, 10 buildings of Wright's designs were realized. This is the William M. Holus Exhibition and Seminar Room. The pierced concrete blocks are inset with colored glass which filters and refracts the sunlight.

ABOVE: Florida Southern University was built largely by unskilled (and unpaid) labor—in this instance, university students earned their tuition by mixing, pouring, and casting the thousands of concrete blocks that Wright designed as the basic module for the buildings.

RIGHT: The university's Annie Pfeiffer Chapel. A hexagon, with its metal spire it is the tallest building of Wright's complex of designs. The walls and structural members of the buildings are constructed of a buff-colored reinforced cast concrete. Wright's ideas regarding ornament as integral to the structure is evident in the contrast of smooth and textured surfaces.

overlooked: like Taliesin West, the campus buildings were largely built with the help of unskilled labor provided by the students of the college themselves. Students earned a portion of their tuition fees by mixing and pouring concrete for the floor slabs, walkways, and the tens of thousands of concrete blocks that served as the basic module for the buildings. Initially, sand from the site itself was used in the concrete mix but the first blocks made immediately crumbled. It turned out that the fertilizer that had been

used in the orange groves over the years made it useless for construction purposes and sand had to be bought in.

In addition to their labor, the students also provided their urine! This was collected daily and mixed with salt and muriatic acid to make a solution that when applied to copper—a material used as a decorative element throughout the campus—rapidly changed it from its bright orange color to subtle blue-green tones.

The years of World War II proved difficult for Wright: there was little new work to be had, yet he wished to keep the Taliesin Fellowship intact. Of the two major commissions during the war period—the enormous project for Crystal Heights in Washington D.C., which was rejected by the local planning commission, and the Community Church in Kansas City, Missouri—only the latter was built and even then Wright refused to list it among his completed works. The building he planned for the congregation of Dr. Burris A. Jenkins was to be a "church of the future" but financial constraints, wartime

shortages of materials, and restrictive building codes greatly compromised the design. As originally planned, this building was the first drive-in church but the scheme for the parking terraces had to be abandoned, as did the rooftop gardens and consequently Wright considered the building his in shape only.

For the plan Wright used a rhombus with two 120-degree angles and two 60-degree angles as the basic unit for the design. Instead of a the "traditional" concrete structure, Gunite—an inexpensive, strong yet lightweight and fireproof concrete material—was sprayed over sheets of corrugated steel which were then sandwiched together to form the walls. This method allowed the walls to be reduced in thickness to a mere 2¾ inches and furthermore it was cheap and fast. The new church was being built because the old one had burned down and the congregation was presently homeless: to build a church from brick or stone would take time and a considerable amount of money which would have to be raised.

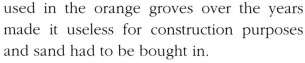

ABOVE LEFT: FLORIDA SOUTHERN UNIVERSITY (1938), Lakeland, Florida. Covered esplanades link the various facilities and administration buildings of the campus.

ABOVE: The interior of the hexagonal-shaped Annie Pfeiffer Chapel, the tallest building on the campus.

RIGHT: Wright's belief in ornament as being integral to architecture is demonstrated in his contrasting of smooth and textured surfaces.

Wright promised Dr. Jenkins a church for $150,000 and, as usual, almost immediately there were problems. Local builders were reluctant to bid on the project, the local authorities refused a building permit—their codes demanded poured concrete foundations and not Wright's proposed rock ballast ones—until finally Wright gave up on the project and any hope of his fees.

A perforated dome was constructed to roof the hexagonal chancel, but the searchlights that Wright had envisaged to illuminate the "Steeple of Light" were not installed until 1994. The completed lighting plan was the work of sculptor-in-light Dale Eldred. On weekends and holidays, the lights, with their

combined illumination power of 1.2 million candles, project through the pierced dome and reach several miles into the sky.

A domestic project of the war years was the magnificent "Eaglefeather," a house for Arch Obler. Situated high on a mountaintop ridge, surrounded by rocky outcrops, with views down to Malibu and the Pacific Ocean, the main house was never built. Parts of the complex, however, were constructed—a stone and wood gatehouse (1940) and a small studio-retreat (1941).

When the end of the war finally came in 1945, Wright was already 78 years old. At an age when most people are slowing down, Wright was gearing up to a new period of activity. Although very few projects had been built during the hostilities, he had nevertheless been busy with plans for projects. The Lowell and Agnes Walter House in Quasqueton, Iowa had been designed in 1942 but construction was delayed until 1948. However in 1945, Wright published the design he referred to as a "glass house" in

OPPOSITE AND ABOVE: THE COMMUNITY CHRISTIAN CHURCH (1940), Kansas City, Missouri. Designed as a "church of the future," wartime restrictions on finances and materials compromised Wright's original plans. The dome of the chancel roof is perforated and searchlights create a "steeple of light," dramatic beams of light which reach several miles into the sky.

TOP LEFT: Detail of Wright's free standing metal sculpture for the church, based on intersecting cross forms.

the *Ladies' Home Journal.* The 11-acre site includes the main house, a two-story boathouse, an outdoor hearth, and an entrance gate. The main living area is a 900-

RIGHT AND OPPOSITE: THE GEORGE ABLIN HOUSE (1958),
Bakersfield, California. Based on a modified triangular module,
the walls of the Ablin House are concrete blocks and include
perforated window screens. The house also contains many fine
examples of Wright's free standing wood furniture, including
geometric wooden "light tower" lamps (Right).

ABOVE: Pierced concrete blocks set with glass form the
masonry core housing the Ablins' kitchen area.

square foot combined living room, dining
alcove, and conservatory, and three exterior
glass walls offer dramatic views of the
Wapsipinicon River and the valley floor. The
interior garden of the conservatory area is
provided with natural light by a central
clerestory and skylight. Extending from an
angle from the main living area is a wing
housing the bedrooms, bathrooms (Pullman
type modules installed as units), utility
rooms, and a carport. The heated floor slab
is concrete, as is the roof with its broad overhanging eaves designed to support a rooftop
garden. Inside, the board-and-batten walls
are executed in walnut and all the furnishings were carried out to Wright's designs.

The projects to be undertaken in the immediate post-war years also included the Unitarian Meeting House in Madison, Wisconsin, and a house for Mrs. Clinton Walker at Carmel, California. Commissioned in 1946, the Unitarian Meeting House—which Wright described as a hilltop "country church"—took five years to build and exceeded by three and a half times the initial budget of $60,000, even though most of labor came from the volunteer workforce of the congregation itself. Constructed of more than 1,000 tons of rough cut limestone, the congregation carted the building materials from a quarry 30 miles away. Wright, too, had a personal involvement in the building apart from its design: his own parents had been among the earliest First Unitarian Society members and he had officially joined the organization in 1938. For the plans, Wright accepted a minimal fee, offered the assistance of the Taliesin fellows and apprentices, and helped to raise funds for the construction by giving two lectures.

The design of the meeting house is based on a diamond module and the geometric form is repeated in the incised pattern on the concrete floor. The meeting house, however, is dominated by the steep, prow-like roof of welted copper that rises to a pointed gable over the pulpit and choir loft (which proved to be too small to house a choir of any size and now houses organ pipes!). The audi-

ABOVE: THE ARCH OBLER GATEHOUSE (1940), Malibu, California. Part of the spectacular project for "Eaglefeather," the main house was never built. Only this, the stone and wood gatehouse, and a small studio-retreat were constructed.

ABOVE RIGHT: THE UNITARIAN MEETING HOUSE (1947), Madison, Wisconsin. Describing the meeting house as a hilltop "country church" to be built of stone and wood, Wright used a diamond module to give the building its most distinctive feature, the copper-clad roof.

RIGHT: THE MRS. CLINTON WALKER HOUSE (1948), Carmel, California. A variation on the Usonian House, the Walker House appears to be part of the rocky coastline itself.

torium and adjacent hearth room can, by contrast, accommodate 340 people and a loggia leads to the west living room where social functions are held. For both the auditorium and hearth room Wright designed collapsible benches and tables and at the meeting house's dedication in August 1951 gave an address on "Architecture as Religion" from the pulpit of the church. whose roof he described as "hands joined in prayer."

While most of the small domestic commissions of the post-war period were carried out under Wright's supervision by senior members of the Taliesin Fellowship, occasionally Wright took a particular interest in a house whose site interested him. This was the case with the house on a rocky stretch of beach at Carmel for Mrs. Clinton Walker. Situated overlooking Monterey Bay, the house has a "floating" blue-colored metal roof. In keeping with a coastal theme, the pointed prow-like form of the stone terrace makes the house look remarkably like a boat about to put to sea. Quite small when built— only 1,200 square feet including the car-

port—Wright used a variation on the Usonian plan with the living-dining room organized around a fireplace, a kitchen core, and, off this, a galleried wing which contained three bedrooms and baths. The plan is based on a module of four-foot interlocking equilateral triangles put together rather like a jigsaw puzzle. An almost unbroken band of casement windows provides views across the ocean and, ingeniously, the horizontal mullions of the windows are corbelled one above the other in a way that allows sections of the windows to be opened downwards, rather than outwards, thus stopping winds and sea spray being blown into the house.

A late California house for George C. Ablin from 1958 also uses a triangular module. The pink walls of this house are concrete block and include patterned perforated block for windows. The low pitched, wood-shingled gable roofs extend outwards to provide shade for the glass walls, terraces, and the entry walk. Leading to the central core of entry room, living room, dining room, and high-ceilinged kitchen is a covered walkway.

From the central core, two wings extend housing bedrooms and a study in one, and children's playroom, and bedrooms in the other. Inside, the house is furnished with examples of Wright's free standing wooden furniture.

In the years after World War II, Wright frequently elaborated on his theme of the Usonian House. Though always arranged around a tight compact masonry core, the houses were often enlarged and loosely spread out over their sites. In design, the house for Robert Berger in San Anselmo, California reworks the 1930s Usonian House.

The fireplace and kitchen workspace make up the central masonry core. Off to one side is the living room, to the other is the bedroom wing. Outside, the low-pitched roof extends over the glass walls of the house encased in heavy, form-built walls of local rock and concrete. Extending from the living room is a concrete and stone, parapeted, walled terrace in the form of a ship's prow.

In the Zimmerman House in New Hampshire, brick, cast concrete, and cypress are used to create a house that is sited diagonally on a one-acre plot. The street facade is dominated by a solid masonry facade pierced by a high, continuous band of windows. In contrast, the garden facade is made of floor-to-ceiling glass, mitered at the corners. in addition to the house, Wright also designed the landscape, all of the free-standing and built-in furniture, and he even

selected the textiles and family's tableware. The internal organization of space, with variations in ceiling height, the use of built in furniture, and the continuous concrete floor slab make the Zimmerman House appear much larger than its actual 1,458 square feet. When the Zimmermans first contacted Wright they had expressed their wish for a house that was an expression of their personal way of life and Wright responded with the design that he called "a classic Usonian." In 1952, the Zimmermans wrote again to Wright telling him that their house was "the most beautiful house in the world."

ABOVE: THE ISADORE J. AND LUCILLE ZIMMERMAN HOUSE (1950), Manchester, New Hampshire. A "classic" Usonian House in brick, cast concrete, and cypress, the Zimmermans claimed their house to be the "most beautiful in the world."

RIGHT, CENTER RIGHT, AND FAR RIGHT: In addition to designing the free standing and built-in furniture, Wright also selected the family's tableware and textiles.

TOP RIGHT: THE ROBERT BERGER HOUSE (1950), San Anselmo, California. Wright even provided the family dog with its own Usonian kennel.

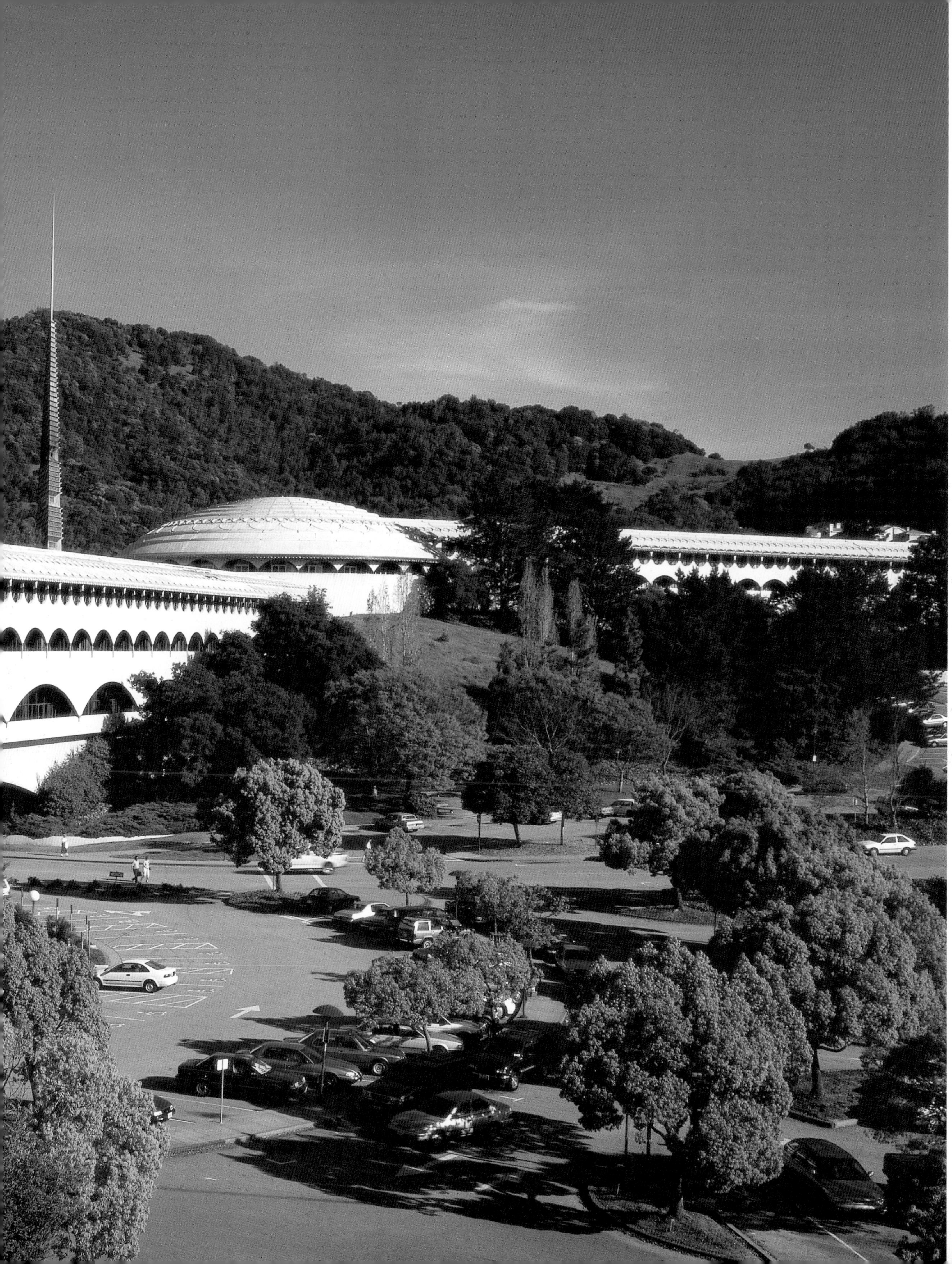

THE GREAT COMMISSIONS

THE GREAT COMMISSIONS

Frank Lloyd Wright produced a vast body of work; his residential architecture provided many of the models still used for suburban architecture across America. Yet in addition to the domestic projects—the single family houses of the Prairie period, the Californian textile-block houses, the Usonian Houses, and the more spectacular commissions for his wealthiest clients—Wright also undertook a wide range of commercial and industrial projects throughout his career: the Larkin Building, the Midway Gardens complex, the Imperial Hotel in Tokyo, the S.C. Johnson and Sons Inc. Administration

ABOVE AND RIGHT: THE S.C. JOHNSON AND SON ADMINSTRATIVE BUILDING (1936), Racine, Wisconsin. Wright's major large commission between the wars, the design reused many ideas from his plans for The Capital Journal's building in Salem, Oregon, including the "dendriform" columns of the great work room (Right).

PREVIOUS PAGE: MARIN COUNTY CIVIC CENTER (1957), San Rafael, California. The 880-foot long Hall of Justice bridges the valley between the hills of the site.

Building and Research Tower, and the Solomon R. Guggenheim Museum as well as temples, civic centers, and a theater, all of which are landmarks in the history of American architecture.

The Larkin Company Administration Building remains one of Wright's most important works—even though it was demolished in 1950—since it not only represented a new architectural form but was also a radical concept of what an office should be. In his domestic architecture Wright had demonstrated his commitment to the therapeutic value of space and light, and he wished to introduce these qualities into an office building. This led him to propose an arrangement which, while it has since been widely accepted in office design, at the time must have appeared revolutionary.

Unlike many of the other big mail order companies of the day, the Larkin

Company manufactured the products that it sold and distributed. Its company literature boasted that its factories covered 60 acres of floor space in downtown Buffalo and that it was the world's largest manufacturer of soaps, perfumes, and toilet preparations which were sent directly from the factory to the home user without middlemen. Because the goods were shipped by rail, factories needed to be sited near railway lines. But because the trains were coal-powered, the factory sites were dark, dirty, and noisy. When Wright was commissioned to design the new administration building, he was shown the available plot of land: a trapezium-shaped site a mile east of Buffalo, in a semi-industrial neighborhood. It was bordered on one side by the New York Central railroad line and on the other two sides by streets full of horse-drawn vehicles. In response to this site, Wright conceived a plan for a building that was totally sealed off from its surroundings and that would provide facilities for executives and department heads and for the 1,800 clerical employees who dealt with the thousands of pieces of customer mail that arrived each day.

The directors of the Larkin Company held progressive views concerning the treatment of employees: picnics, weekly concerts, educational incentives, and profit-sharing schemes were some of the employee benefits on offer. The Larkin executives believed that such benefits and a clean, safe, and attractive working environment meant increased staff productivity and these two considerations, the success of the business and the well being of the staff, dominated both the planning of the building and its decorative sculptural details, which included fountains and numerous inscriptions.

Frank Lloyd Wright created a six and a half-story courtyard building as the main factory and a smaller annex to house most of the company's support activities. The main structure was based on an open plan, with a series of tall galleries located around a central, vertical court that was top-lit by rooflights. Around the exterior wall, windows provided additional light. The building was inward-looking, with the glass-roofed central hall rising its full height with office floors encircling it.

Because the Larkin Company was a mail order business, the system for dealing with mail that had been established in the 1890s needed to be incorporated into the design of the new building. The mail was delivered via an arched opening on the Swan Street side of the building to a receiving area in the semi-basement where it was loaded onto elevators and taken to the third floor. Here, it was sorted into "state groups": the Buffalo office handled mail for 10 states east of the Mississippi River while a second office in Illinois handled the mail from the western states. The mail from each state was distributed to four work groups accommodated on the fourth floor, three on the third floor, two on the second, and one on the first.

Wright did not, therefore, build an office full of space for the Larkin Company to fill as it wished; the design was carefully detailed and worked out in close collaboration with the clients. Furthermore, the circulation of the mail throughout the Larkin Building reflected both the company's organization and Wright's own ideal of "organic" architecture. Once the mail left the third floor, it went downward through the building (except for that delivered to the fourth floor). This vertical pattern of flow Wright would later re-use in his scheme for the Solomon R. Guggenheim Museum in New York in 1959.

The stairs of the main building were separate from it: they were housed in semi-attached towers at the outer corners and elevators were placed near the entrance and reception area. The stair towers had a dual function: as well as providing a communication network, they also housed the ducts which served as air inlets for the ventilation system. Room for food preparation and

dining was on the fifth floor, the last full story of the main block while elevator machinery and furnaces were housed in the basement.

Because the founder of the company, John D. Larkin, had been a witness to the devastation of the Chicago fire of 1871, he insisted that all Larkin buildings be constructed to be fireproof. For the Larkin Company Wright designed a steel-framed building clad in brick, inside and out. Exterior details were carried out in red sandstone, the entrance doors, windows, and skylights in glass. Floors, desk tops, and filing cabinet tops and sides were covered in magnesite for sound absorption. This was a chalky, grey-colored substance that was mixed, poured, and troweled like cement. For the floors, magnesite was poured over a layer of felt to give a degree of resilience or "bounce" and the same material was used in the sculptural decorations of the piers that surrounded the light court. All the office furniture in the main block was designed in metal by Wright to be integral to the overall design. There were three different types of desk, and four different types of chair (including a three-legged chair that was so unstable that it became known among Larkin employees as "the suicide chair"). Chairs and desks were made of folded and punched steel riveted together in a manner similar to that used in the steel frame of the building itself and were fabricated by the Van Dorn Iron Works of Cleveland, Ohio. The Larkin Building also contained the first use of double glazing, the first use of modular metal and glass fittings, and the first use of the hanging bathroom partition and wall-hung lavatories. Today, all that remains of the building are fragments of the foundation

Do Not
Enter

SC Johnson
WAX

walls but in his autobiography Frank Lloyd Wright took some satisfaction in learning how difficult—and how expensive—the Larkin Building was to destroy!

A similar fate was to befall the two other major projects of Wright's early career: the Midway Gardens in Chicago (1913–14) and the Imperial Hotel in Tokyo (1915).

In the late summer of 1913 Wright was approached by Edward Waller Jr. with a commission to create an entertainment center on Cottage Green Avenue in Chicago. The complex was of the kind then popular in Europe and, given Chicago's large German population, it was thought that an open air restaurant and pleasure gardens would prove equally popular when transplanted to the New World. In order to make it financially successful, it was decided that the Midway Gardens would be open all year round, with a winter garden, bar, and indoor dance hall. This was to be no mere "beer garden" but a well-built, permanent structure providing the highest quality food, drink, and entertainment—including opera, ballet, and symphony orchestras. All that was lacking was the money to build! The budget called for an expenditure of some $350,000: Waller and his associates raised $65,000 with the remainder to be made by selling stock in the project. Wright took most of his fees in stock in the Chicago Midway Gardens Corporation, which would eventually prove to be worthless. Nevertheless, Wright was happy with the plans he devised for the complex, a fantasy of brick and patterned concrete blocks that enclosed a vast space on several different levels. The articulation of space was such that in parts of the building it was impossible for the visitor to tell whether he was inside or out, a happy confusion that was augmented by the use of artificial lights which turned night into day.

In addition to designing the buildings themselves, Wright was also responsible for the design of all the furnishings—right down to the tableware, the designs for which were based on Vienna Secessionist abstract principles, and motifs that Wright had seen during his visit to Europe to prepare the Wasmuth folio of his work. Sculptors Richard Bok and Alfonso Iannelli contributed works in a variety of materials to Wright's designs.

Regrettably, the Midway Gardens lasted for only two years in the form intended by Waller and Wright. A number of factors contributed to its demise. It is possible that the German precedents for its establishment may have been unfortunate on the eve of World War I but its failure was more likely due to the fact that it continued to be debt-ridden. In 1916 it was sold to a brewery, which hoped to transform it into a more successful, but less culturally highbrow, beer garden, but even this prospect was dashed when the Volsted Act was passed in 1920 and years of Prohibition followed. In 1929, the Midway Gardens was demolished, though once again Wright is said to have had some consolation in the fact that the structures were so well built that the contractor hired to raze the building went broke during the process. While some portions and sculptures were rescued by Wright's admirers (most were destined to be used as garden ornaments) other portions were unceremoniously dumped in Lake Michigan to help build a breakwater.

Like Midway Gardens, the Imperial Hotel in Tokyo was a large complex that was unified by Wright's decorative scheme, which included the designs for all the interior details—furniture, carpets, and textiles, ceramics, and silverware. In 1913 Wright and Mamah Cheney Borthwick had visited Japan: while Wright asserted that the trip was at the invitation of the Emperor, it is more likely that its real purpose was to purchase Japanese prints for re-sale to American collectors. During the course of the visit, however, Wright was contacted by representatives of the Emperor who informed him of the Court's wish to replace the old Imperial

Hotel—built in the 19th century by German investors—with a new, de luxe building which would attract foreign visitors to the city. The commission was important to Wright for two reasons: first, it gave him the opportunity to design on the grand scale, something that had been denied him until then; second, it offered him the opportunity to begin his personal life afresh with his new companion Miriam Noel, after the tragic death of Mamah Cheney in the Taliesin fire in the summer of 1914.

Wright had earlier prepared plans for a temporary annex to house guests in need of accommodation before the hotel proper was complete. By the time he arrived in

Tokyo, the annex was complete and a studio-penthouse served as Wright's workspace. Construction of the Imperial Hotel began in 1916 and continued through 1922. While it might be expected that Wright designed a hotel in "the Japanese style," this is far from the truth. In fact, the Imperial Hotel shared some characteristics with the Midway Gardens, in particular in the Mayan themes that he had been investigating in the German Warehouse and in "Hollyhock House." For building materials, Wright used oya— Japanese lava stone—a stone rarely used by the Japanese for construction because it was highly porous and incapable of being water-proofed. In addition, terracotta was used on

ABOVE LEFT: S.C JOHNSON AND SON ADMINISTRATION BUILDING (1936), Racine, Wisconsin. Wright's major non-domestic commission of the inter-war period was conceived with the intention of improving the working conditions of the employees.

ABOVE: As in the earlier Larkin Company Building, for the Johnson Wax Company Wright designed the interior furnishings including the desks, which although extensively modified for contemporary business practices, are still in use today.

the exterior and interior arcades of the building to give a rich mosaic-like effect, similar to that achieved at Midway Gardens.

While the public rooms of the hotel were vast in size, the bedrooms were rather small. However, because so much of the furniture in them was "built-in," the overall effect was said to be rather snug, like a ship's

cabin. In designing the hotel and its furnishings, Wright created a cohesive unity through the use of geometric forms, such as the hexagonal backs of the chairs, the shape of which was repeated in the table tops and in the ceiling decoration of the central lounge. The character of the Imperial Hotel, however, was determined largely by its structure. Huge piers and composite walls of brick and concrete created areas in which loggias and balconies played a major role, while water-filled pools and planters full of greenery added to the "natural" dimension.

The chief fame of the building springs from its having survived the great earthquake of 1923, which all but devastated Tokyo and Yokohama—the water from the pools was used to douse the fires burning in adjoining buildings! Furthermore, the hotel remained largely undamaged through World War II, although during the early years of the U.S. occupation of Japan, the hotel was altered by the U.S. military, who used it as their Tokyo headquarters. In 1968, the hotel was demolished, but the entrance lobby was dismantled and reconstructed in 1976 at the Meiji Village, a museum to the west of Tokyo.

The major non-domestic commission of the inter-war period, the S.C. Johnson Administration Building was, like the Larkin Building, conceived with the intention of improving the working conditions of the employees. The Johnson Company had become well-known for its interests in the welfare of its staff: it had been a pioneer in the introduction of paid holidays, the eight-hour working day and profit-sharing. When in 1936 Hib Johnson, the third generation of his family to run the company, saw that a new administration building was required, it was his wish that the employees gained improved working conditions as well as increased space. (The building was also to incorporate a theater and squash courts.)

The design of the administration building reused ideas Wright had envisaged using for the construction of a newspaper building, for *The Capital Journal*, in Salem, Oregon, which was never built. The most notable "borrowing" was the concrete and steel columns he had designed to support duplex apartments above a huge, two-story high hall. This would have contained the newspaper's printing presses at ground level and glass-encased offices on the mezzanine level overlooking the presses. Wright called the columns "dendriform" or "tree-shaped" although they are in fact upside-down trees—the narrowest part of the column is at the base and they increase in size to vast circular "roots," which are joined to other "roots." These circular caps, sometimes described as "lily pads" do not support the roof, but actually are the roof. In the spaces between the columns in the administration building, light is admitted through Pyrex glass tubes, while the 128-foot by 208-foot "great workroom" below contains nothing except the office furniture (designed by Wright) the staff needed to carry out their work. The use of translucent glass tubing instead of transparent window glass was unprecedented and not without problems. While there was no doubt about its beauty and the quality of light it provided, when the sun struck it at an angle it produced a blinding glare. Furthermore, in rainy weather, it leaked! Despite numerous attempts to solve the problem, in the end the rooftop tubing was covered over with a second roof and artificial lighting was introduced between the roof and the tubes to simulate daylight.

The perimeter walls of the Johnson Administration Building, freed from any support role, extended the theme of the ceiling design by terminating in an upper band of glass tubes which ran continuously around the building. The bricks used in both the interior and exterior walls were custom-made in 200 different shapes to produce the required curves and angles of the building's rounded corners. Between the bricks, the horizontal mortar joints were raked to preserve the streamlined effect. Heating was provided by special wrought-iron steam pipes under the concrete floor and the building was fully air-conditioned with vents provided by the cylindrical "nostrils" emerging at roof level. As in the Larkin Building, the central main entrance in the Johnson Administration Building was not on the street facade. Here, for efficiency, Wright placed the main entrance at the rear, next to the carport. The Johnson Administration Building successfully combined Wright's beliefs in organic structures and his acknowledgement of the machine.

Although Hib Johnson frequently asserted through the long process of building the Administration Building that he would never again employ Wright on any project, he was in fact to commission Wright on two other occasions: for his own "Wingspread" (1937) and for a second building for the Johnson Company, a research tower.

Wright called the Johnson House "Wingspread" because the plan consisted of four wings extended in a pinwheel fashion from a high-ceilinged, polygonal central space (which Wright likened to a wigwam) housing an enormous chimney with five fireplaces on two levels. At the point where the chimney emerged through the sloping, tiled roof Wright placed a small glass observatory designed to serve as a sort of tree house for the Johnson children.

At 14,000 square feet, "Wingspread" is an exceedingly large "mansion"—even though Wright referred to it as his "last Prairie House." The focal point of the living space remains the "sacred hearth," the "heart" of the home. Inside the warm brick and oak tones are enriched by light from three bands of clerestory windows, set into a circle round the roof. The library area features Wright's built-in furniture: sofa, coffee tables, and octagonal ottomans. A circular staircase leads to the mezzanine from which the observation deck is accessed via a metal spiral-staircase.

In 1943 Hib Johnson returned to Wright with the commission for new quarters for the company's research and development division. Using a circular yet rectilinear theme, the Research Tower echoes the central support principles of the dendriform columns of the Administration Building. Like a strong tree, the 14-story tower forms a central core from which reinforced concrete slabs are cantilevered to form alternating square floors and circular balconies contained in a skin of brick and glass. A central shaft contains the stairwell, elevator shafts, and the electrical and mechanical systems and the whole tower is linked to the main building by a covered bridge. The additional storys to the east of the tower, based roughly on Wright's plans, were constructed in 1961, and in 1978 two black granite sculptures (representing the figures of Nakoma and Nakomis that Wright had designed in 1924 for an unexecuted project in Wisconsin) were installed in the Research Tower courtyard.

With the Research Tower, Wright demonstrated that he was no longer confined to horizontal structures and both the Administration Building and the Research Tower brought the geometric form of the circle into Wright's architecture as a positive force for the first time. The discovery of the potential of circular geometry was to inspire Wright to create an entire new vocabulary of architectural forms, which would culminate in the circle-spiral of the Guggenheim Museum.

Earlier, in 1929, Wright had proposed an apartment block in the form of a vertical structure, the St. Mark's Tower in the Bowery project. In 1956 his idea came to be built in the form of the Price Tower in Bartlesville, Oklahoma. When Harold C. Price approached Frank Lloyd Wright with the commission to design a building for his oil pipeline construction firm, he had in mind a two or three-story building with parking for around 10 trucks. Wright rejected the concept as inefficient and several months later

LEFT AND BELOW: THE PRICE COMPANY TOWER (1952), Bartlesville, Oklahoma. All the furnishings were custom designed for the building including those for the apartments and for Price's 19th floor office. Like the tower itself, the furniture and the decorative motifs are based on a diamond module of 30-degree and 60-degree triangles.

presented Price with drawings for a 19-story, 37,000-square foot multi-use tower, which would function as the corporate headquarters with additional space for apartments and offices. Wright described the tower as "a needle on the prairie" and a "tree escaped from the forest." The design is, in fact, very tree-like, for its concrete floor slabs cantilever like branches from four interior vertical supports of steel-reinforced concrete. The building increases substantially in area from floor to floor as the tower rises, rather like the canopy of a tree. Each glass fronted apartment or office sheds rainwater clear of the floor below. The concrete floor slabs, like branches, are thickest near the supporting shafts and get thinner (to three inches thick) as they "grow" outwards towards the exterior screen walls. The exterior walls are ornamental screens because they have been freed of their load-bearing function. The outer enclosing screens are made of glass and 20-inch copper louvers, which shade the inner window surfaces of gold-tinted glass.

At 186 feet tall, the Price Tower is made up of a two-story base, and a 17-story tower. The supporting members are located inside the building and carry the elevators. Most of the upper floors contain four diamond-shaped units allocated for use as offices or apartments. Each space is separated from the others as all look outwards: the exterior walls of each apartment and office are entirely of glass set into metal framing. According to Wright, in *The Story of the Tower* which was published by the Horizon Press in 1956, the building was so placed that the sun shone only on one wall at a time and the narrow, upright blades or mullions, which project nine inches, created shadows on the glass surface as the sun moved and thus cut out extreme glare and heat.

The southwest quadrant is a little different in layout: here there is a separate entrance and elevator to serve the eight, two-story offices. The 19th floor—not a full quadrant—was reserved for Price's office and a rooftop garden overlooking the city. In addition to designing the mural on the 17th floor, Wright also designed the built-in desk and the glass mural in Price's office.

LEFT AND BELOW LEFT: THE PRICE COMPANY TOWER (1952), Bartlesville, Oklahoma. The diamond modular motif is repeated in the decoration throughout the tower. It can be seen scored on the floors and in the murals designed by Wright for the 17th and 19th floors. The top floor which housed Price's office was not a full quadrant and benefited from a rooftop garden overlooking the city.

RIGHT: THE LINDHOLM SERVICE STATION (1957), Cloquet, Minnesota. Proudly announcing the fact that this is the only service station design by Wright that has been built, the Lindholm Service Station included elements that would be incorporated into many later service stations.

Completed at a cost of approximately $2.5 million, at least $1 million more than originally budgeted, the tower was an immediate success and provided a large amount of free publicity for the Price Company. Price himself was evidently happy with his building and commissioned Wright to design two family homes in Phoenix and in Bartlesville. Following the completion of Price Tower, Wright appeared on television and he pointed out the beauty of his tower—particularly when compared to the Phillips Petroleum Company office buildings which were also in the neighborhood. The Phillips Petroleum people took this attack on their buildings in good spirits and even Price wrote to Wright asking him to hold his tongue, reminding him that he had to do business with Phillips and that one day, Phillips might want a building from the very man who insulted their architectural integrity!

While no commission for a corporate headquarters for the Phillips Petroleum Company was ever forthcoming, Wright was commissioned by them to design a service station! Always a great fan of automobiles and the owner of several, Wright first began working on the design for a prefabricated gasoline station in the 1920s and the Lindholm Station in the Minnesota town of Cloquet is a variation on Wright's prototype design. When opened, the gas station attracted a great deal of attention and customers— the pump sales set a new record for Phillips 66! Still open for business today on Route 33 and Cloquet Avenue, the design includes a

friend Boris Blai, who had taught at Florida Southern College in the 1940s and who had become a close friend of Frank Lloyd Wright. Cohen contacted Wright and sent him his sketch. Normally Wright would have rejected outright anyone who he believed simply wanted him to transform their ideas into a building but on this occasion he agreed to meet the Rabbi to discuss the project.

The plans and elevations for the synagogue revealed that Wright had indeed translated Cohen's desire into a building: a tabernacle also implied a tent and Wright designed a building whose shape was certainly tent-like. Three huge steel and concrete uprights, sheathed in copper (although later, aluminum was substituted), rise 117 feet into the air and form a tripod from which sloping walls of translucent plastic hang. The tripod rests on a cradle of reinforced concrete from which three wings spring out, reversing the angle to absorb the outward thrust of the tripod's legs. The structure's roughly hexagonal plan, according to Wright, mirrored the shape of cupped hands—the cupped hands of God in which the congregation safely rests—while the ramps of broad, deep stairs with shallow risers leading from the entrance to the main sanctuary are intended to suggest the ascent of Mount Sinai. The 100-foot high pyramidal, translucent roof thus takes on the form of the mountain itself, and the light which filters through its walls symbolizes the divine gift of the law. The main sanctuary can accommodate 1,100 people in seating arranged in triangular sections around two sides of the projecting pulpit. The pulpit, or Bimah, by tradition is the platform from which the rabbi and cantor conduct the service and is generally in a low place, in the middle of the auditorium

60-foot illuminated rooftop pylon and an upper level observation lounge while the 32-foot cantilevered copper canopy was designed to hold overhead hoses, eliminating the need for pump islands (although fire regulations led to this part of the scheme being abandoned). Although it is the only Wright-designed station to be built, details such as the V-shaped canopy and the canted windows were incorporated into other Phillips Petroleum stations.

The St. Mark's Tower in the Bowery, which was the basis of the design for Price Tower, was also the design which inspired the form of Wright's 1954 commission for the Beth Sholom Synagogue in Elkins Park, Philadelphia. The synagogue, with its complex symbolism, is the result of close collaboration with the commissioner, Rabbi Mortimer J. Cohen—so much so that the Wright's initial sketches bore Cohen's name

as co-designer. Cohen had been called to be rabbi of Beth Sholom—the congregation had chosen the name "House of Peace" to celebrate the end of World War I—in 1920 and the first synagogue, a red-brick and limestone Georgian-style building, was dedicated in 1922. As the congregation grew in size and prosperity, Cohen realised that a larger synagogue was needed and in the early 1950s land was purchased at Elkins Park, where a school and community center was built. When informed that the congregation was prepared to raise half a million dollars for a new synagogue, Cohen set down in sketches exactly what the ideal synagogue should be. First, there was to be no reference to earlier architectural styles and, second, he wanted the synagogue to be the embodiment of the idea of the Tabernacle that God had instructed Moses to build for the wandering Jews. Cohen was urged to contact Wright by his

of a synagogue. This tradition was not strictly adhered to as Wright argued that the lowest point in the auditorium was needed for seats, and every seat he could provide would pay for the synagogue. The 40-foot high concrete monolith which represents the stone tablets given to Moses forms the backdrop to the Ark containing the 10 Torah scrolls, one for each of the commandments. Cohen had reminded Wright also that the Ark had to be made of wood because metal was forbidden material (as it was a symbol of war) and that it must always be approached by steps—never fewer than three steps and as many as 12, as in the ancient temple in Jerusalem. Over the Ark Wright had argued for a representation of the Burning Bush as a feature of the lighting. Cohen, however, was against the concept and sent Wright his design for the triangular aluminum and glass sculpture "Wings," the colors of which symbolize divine emanations.

In addition to the main sanctuary, the Beth Sholom Synagogue also has a smaller sanctuary which can accommodate 250 worshippers, lounges, offices, and meeting rooms, all of which can be accessed from the main entrance. Not surprisingly, Wright also found room for two further features: his beloved fireplaces.

The tent-like structure of Beth Sholom was a form to which Wright returned in designs completed shortly before his death for the Pilgrim Congregational Church in Redding, California. In addition to the tent-like sanctuary, the project consisted of an adjacent chapel, church offices, and a fellowship hall. The building structure has a rough-cut stone and concrete base, over which a metal roof is suspended from rows of high-pitched pre-cast concrete supports—rather like tent poles. The plan is based on a triangular module, evident in the tiles of the floor and in the details of the wooden interior ceiling. Completed in 1963, the church still lacks the intended central

stone tower surmounted by a thin metal spire which would have unified the Structure's three main "wings."

The basic triangle, symbolizing the Christian Trinity, was also essential to both the form and concept of the earlier First Christian Church in Phoenix, Arizona. The building also restates Wright's belief that the modern church should be without historical references. Although not completed until 1972, 13 years after Wright's death, the church sanctuary had originally been designed in 1950 as a university chapel for the Southwest Christian Seminary, whose president Peyon Canary had commissioned

FAR LEFT: PILGRIM CONGREGATIONAL CHURCH (1958), Redding, California. The tent-like structure that Wright had used in Beth Sholom Synagogue was a form to which he returned shortly before his death in the design for the Pilgrim Congregational Church. The plan is based on Wright's familiar triangular module evident in the winged entrance: 23 triangular steel and concrete pillars support the building while the steel roof is suspended from rows of high-pitched concrete supports—rather like tent poles.

LEFT AND BELOW: THE FIRST CHRISTIAN CHURCH (1950), Phoenix, Arizona. Once again the triangle—symbolic of Christian unity—is the basis of the form and structure of this church. Triangular steel and concrete pillars support the building while the pyramidal roof and 77-foot spire crown a second, narrower range of triangular columns which also frame the clerestory windows. Inside light falls through the spire's colored glass insets onto the floor of the diamond-shaped sanctuary.

BOTTOM LEFT: Frank Lloyd Wright Signature Tile from the First Christian Church (1950), Phoenix, Arizona— the modest mark of a great genius.

Wright to design the chapel, offices, and teaching facilities, a library, theater, and faculty housing for the proposed 80-acre campus. The university was never built but in 1970 members of the congregation approached the Frank Lloyd Wright Foundation with the idea of constructing the 1950 plan for their church. 23 triangular steel and concrete pillars support the building, while a narrower range of triangular columns, which frame the clerestory windows, are crowned by a pyramidal roof and a 77-foot spire. Light filters through colored glass insets in the spire and falls onto the floor of the diamond-shaped sanctuary, which is large enough to seat 1,000 worshippers. the 120-foot, free-standing bell tower has four unequal sides, but has the appearance of being triangular.

By the time the Beth Sholom Synagogue was completed in 1956, Wright was busy at work on another religious building, the Annunciation Greek Orthodox Church in Wauwatosa, Wisconsin. In this building he incorporated the symbols of the Greek Orthodox faith in the plan, essentially a Greek cross circumscribed by a circle. The same device was translated into the decorative elements and appears throughout the sanctuary. Four equally spaced reinforced concrete piers support the domed structure and define the cross on the main floor. Inside, the sanctuary has no interior supports to obstruct the view of the worshippers and no parishioner sits more than 60 feet from the sacristy. A lower level space seats 240 people and also contains a circular banqueting hall connected to an underground classroom. Circular stairs lead to the upper level which seats a further 560 congregants. Light enters the building through semicircular win-

ABOVE AND RIGHT: THE KALITA HUMPHREYS THEATER (1955), Dallas, Texas. The only commissioned theatre ever completed from Frank Lloyd Wright's designs, the reinforced concrete structure was built onto the hillside of a one-acre wooded site. The theater consists of a 127-ton cantilevered cylindrical drum with eight-inch thick walls; the drum contains the 44-foot circular thrust stage (above) with its revolving circular platform. Additional performing space can be provided by the fixed apron, side stages, and two balconies which flank the main stage. Completed after Wright's death under the supervision of Taliesin Architects, the theater was modified to upgrade the lighting and to add new rehearsal spaces.

dows and 325 transparent glass spheres which separate the edge of the upper wall and the domed roof. The dome itself is of concrete but is not fixed to the outer wall; it floats on a bed of thousands of steel bearings contained in the circular channel beam capping the outer wall. Originally the dome was covered in a celestial blue-colored ceramic tile ,which was replaced with a synthetic roofing material. The Annunciation Greek Orthodox Church took two years to complete and was dedicated in 1961.

Sharing a similar floor plan if not function to many of Wright's religious buildings were his numerous projects for theaters. As early as 1915 Wright was at work on an "experimental theater" for Aline Barnsdall; it featured a cycloramic, elevator stage and a minimal separation between the actors and the audience. In 1931 he designed the "New Theater" for Woodstock, New York and a similar theater in 1949 for Hartford, Connecticut. Wright believed that the new theater should free the stage of the tradition-

al proscenium arch and join the actors and audience together in a more unified space. None of these buildings was ever realized. The only commissioned theater ever completed from Wright's designs is the Kalita Humphreys Theater in Dallas, Texas.

In 1955 when he was approached by the Dallas Theater Center's building committee, Wright proposed adapting his design for the "New Theater" for this project. The structure consists of a cylindrical drum containing a 40-foot circular thrust stage, with a revolv-

ing 32-foot center platform. Additional performance space is made available through the use of a fixed apron, side stages, and two balconies flanking the main stage. The eight-inch thick concrete wall of the drum is a cantilevered construction which is supported and anchored to the hillside site by the building's backstage area. The complex also includes dressing rooms on three levels and a spiral ramp which leads to the production workshop areas housed beneath the auditorium. The theater can seat 466 people and

was completed after Wright's death under the supervision of Taliesin Architects.

In the two years before his death in 1959 Wright continued to a astound his admirers and critics alike with the number of projects being undertaken. While Beth Sholom and the Guggenheim Museum were under construction, Wright and his Taliesin Architects were also at work on the Hoffman Auto Showroom in New York, on numerous domestic projects—including an unbuilt project for movie star Marilyn Monroe and her

new husband, playwright Arthur Miller—as well as a complex of buildings for Baghdad commissioned by the King of Iraq.

In 1957 a civic commission allowed Wright to return to the city planning scheme that he had conceived in the mid-1930s: Broadacre. The Marin County Board of Supervisors bought 140 acres of land to the north of San Raphael, California where it intended to house, under one roof, the 13 local government offices scattered throughout the region. Wright was commissioned to develop the master plan for the site; in the same year he presented a design for a 584-foot long Administration Building and an 880-foot long Hall of Justice which would

bridge the valleys between the three adjacent hills of the site. The focal point of the plan was a low dome, 80 feet in diameter and crowned by a 172-foot golden tower (which housed the chimney). Built out of pre-cast and pre-stressed concrete and steel, the construction technique made use of segmentation and expansion joints so that the buildings would withstand significant seismic shocks—the region lies on the famous San Andreas Fault. Originally the central atriums were to be open to the sky, but after Wright's death, practical considerations led to this scheme being replaced by barrel-vaulted skylights. Construction had just begun when Wright died: Wes Peters of Taliesin Architects

ABOVE AND RIGHT: MARIN COUNTY CIVIC CENTER (1957), San Rafael, California. Under design and construction at the time of his death in 1959, the complex of buildings continued Wright's interest in city planning that had been developed in the plans and model for Broadacre City in the mid-1930s. The plans for the civic center included a 584-foot long Administration Building and an 880-foot long Hall of Justice. The focal point and center of the plan is the flattened dome with a 172-foot gold tower (Right) which encases a smokestack.

and Aaron Green, a Wright associate, took over the direction of the project.

The exterior screen walls are divided into arcades and circular openings which from the inside frame the views of the surrounding countryside. The circular motif is continued in the decorative grillwork and in

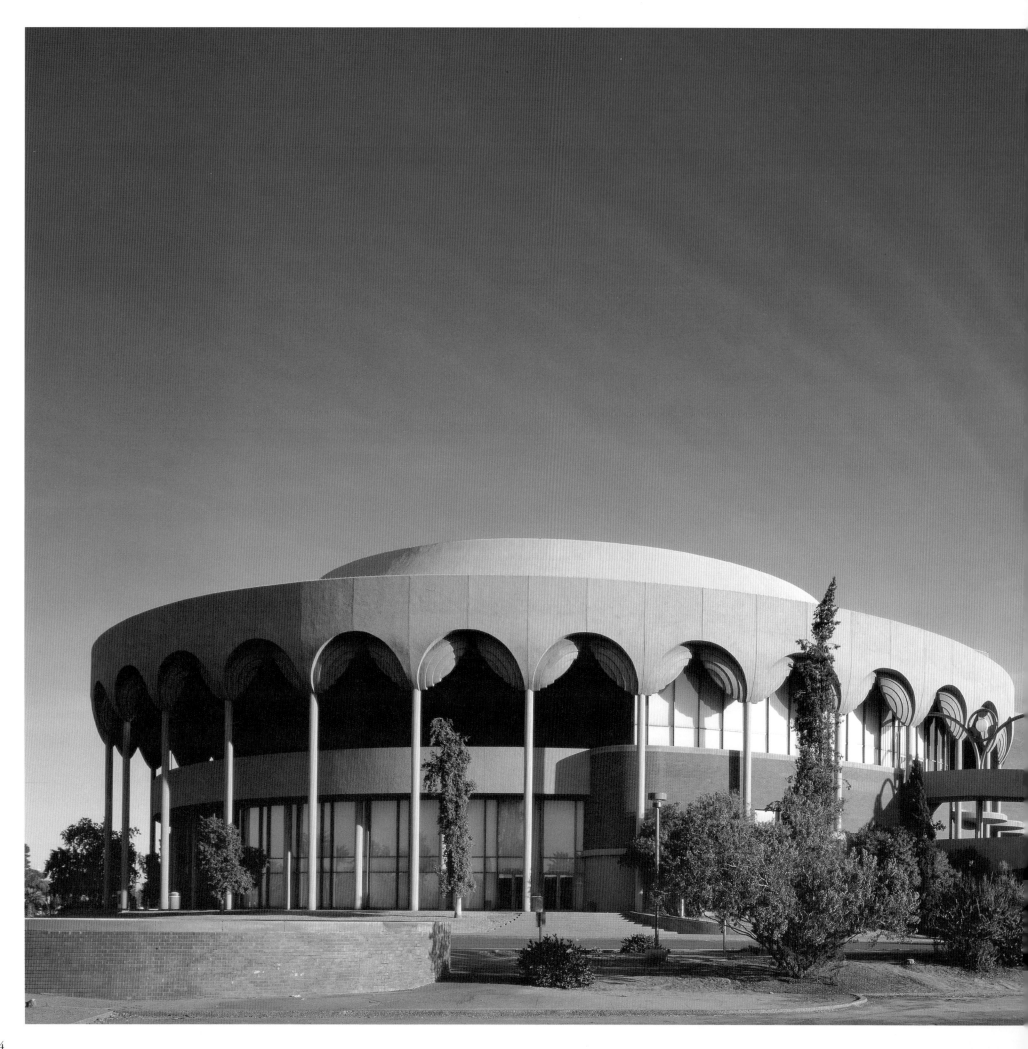

FAR LEFT AND LEFT: GRADY GAMMAGE MEMORIAL AUDITORIUM (1959), Tempe, Arizona. Although Wright had lived in Arizona each winter since 1937, the only civic commission from that state came in the last year of his life. Wright's design for this public space is a circular 3,000-seat center for performing arts with a concert hall, theater, teaching spaces, and offices constructed of steel, cast concrete, and brick. The arcade of 55-foot columns—50 of them—wraps around the facade and supports the concrete shell roof. The circular motif is repeated in the decorative lights of the two 200-foot long pedestrian walkways which provide access to and from the sunken lawns and the parking lot.

The only civic commission that Wright received from the state of Arizona, where he had lived during the winter months at Taliesin West since 1937, came during the last year of his life: a circular 3,000-seat center for the performing arts. The building was commissioned by Grady Gammage, Arizona State University's ninth president and long-term friend of Wright. It was to be sited on the southwest corner of the campus, originally the site of a women's athletic field. An arcade of 50 columns, 55-foot tall, circles the facade and supports the thin shell of the concrete roof. The plan of the auditorium building is actually composed of two circles of unequal size: the larger circle contains the promenades, lobbies, and audience hall. The smaller circle houses the dressing rooms, workshops, teaching areas, and offices as well as the auditorium stage with its 140-foot wide stage and steel acoustic shell, which can be mechanically adjusted to accommodate the sounds of a full orchestra and accompanying choir, or collapsed and stored against the rear wall during theatrical presentations. The seating arrangement follows the European style and does not have radiating aisles. Instead the audience moves to their seats through the 24 doors along the sides and rear of the auditorium. Additional seating is provided by a balcony and grand tier supported by a 145-foot long girder that is not attached to the rear wall of the auditorium and so allows sound to encircle the audience. Two 200-foot long pedestrian bridges—lit by translucent glass globes suspended from metal circles topping overlapping semicircular arches—give access to the

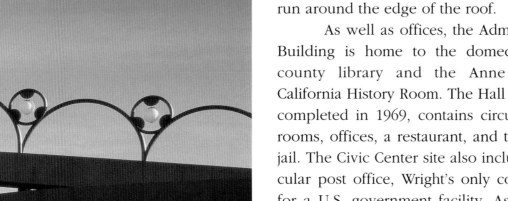

the gold-anodized aluminum spheres that run around the edge of the roof.

As well as offices, the Administration Building is home to the domed, circular county library and the Anne T. Kent California History Room. The Hall of Justice, completed in 1969, contains circular courtrooms, offices, a restaurant, and the county jail. The Civic Center site also includes a circular post office, Wright's only commission for a U.S. government facility. As a whole, Marin County Civic Center can be seen as a direct expression of Wright's view that in a democracy it is the citizen and his activities that count: the interior atriums are public and the auditorium, library, exhibition hall, fairground pavilion, and pleasure lagoon reinforce the sense that this is a citizen's "civic" center rather than a cold, faceless bureaucratic organization of buildings.

GRADY GAMMAGE MEMORIAL AUDITORIUM

LEFT: GRADY GAMMAGE MEMORIAL AUDITORIUM (1959), Tempe, Arizona. The theme of circular motifs seen on the outside of the auditorium is continued in the interior decoration.

RIGHT: SOLOMON R. GUGGENHEIM MUSEUM (1956), New York, New York. Wright had called the gradually opening cast concrete form of the building a "ziggurat." Inside, the main gallery is composed of a quarter mile long cantilevered ramp which curves continuously as it rises through 75 feet to the glass-domed skylight of the roof.

building from the adjacent lawn and sunken parking lot. Neither Gammage nor Wright lived long enough to see the building finally completed in 1964. Once again, Wes Peters of Taliesin Architects was largely responsible for overseeing the construction, the engineering, and much of the interior design.

Despite the complexity and beauty of all of these late works, it is the Solomon R. Guggenheim Museum which will always be considered the ultimate symbol of Wright's oeuvre, even though it was not his last work. The driving forces behind the idea of the museum were Solomon R. Guggenheim and Hilla Rebay. Guggenheim, who had commissioned the museum in 1943, had become a millionaire from a copper-mining business and had an interest in collecting of Old Masters. Then Baroness Hildegarde Rebay von Ehrenweisen, better known as the painter Hilla Rebay, painted a portrait of Guggenheim and introduced her patron to the works of European non-objective painters: soon he was amassing a collection of works by artists like Chagall, Kandinsky, Klee, Mondrian, Delaunay, and Lazlo Moholy-Nagy. Guggenheim was then faced with the problem of where to house his collection. Since many other millionaire patrons and collectors—Freer, Mellon, Huntington, and Frick—were busy establishing museums of their collections, Guggenheim followed suit and Rebay set about getting the project off the ground. Contacting Moholy-Nagy, Rebay asked him to recommend an architect: he replied with a list which included Le Corbusier, Walter Gropius, Richard Neutra,

Marcel Breuer, Alvar Aalto, and, of course, himself! Given that the United States was at war at this time (and Rebay herself was still a German citizen), Rebay shrewdly realized that an American-born architect would be more appropriate and the choice fell naturally to Frank Lloyd Wright—even though it appears that Rebay believed that he was dead! Still alive and in remarkably good health at age 76, Wright was contacted by Rebay, who was invited to Taliesin—even though Wright thought her to be a man and also extended the invitation to Rebay's wife! In the end Wright visited Guggenheim (who was already 82 years old and died in 1949 without seeing his museum) and Rebay in New York; in June 1943 he signed a contract agreeing to design a museum. The major problem that Rebay and Guggenheim faced was finding a suitable site: 13 years were to pass before one was found. Eventually one of two parcels of land facing Fifth Avenue was purchased, giving the museum the entire block front except for a house on the corner of 89th Street. In the meantime, Wright was busy designing the gradually opening, cast concrete, upside-down spiral "ziggurat." The design is purely sculptural: here there are no surface embellishments and the streamlined exterior sets the pattern of wall and spaces that correspond to the changes in level in the interior. Inside the main gallery, a cantilevered ramp, a quarter of a mile long, curves around the inside of the building as it rises 75 feet to the roof. More than the triangle, hexagon, or circle that had been the module for many earlier works, for Wright the spiral was the most exciting architectural form because it existed in three dimensions and because an expanding spiral—as in the case of the Guggenheim Museum—seemed to defy gravity.

Works of art in the museum are displayed on the ground floor and in 74 circular bays which line the walls of the ramp. Flooding the building with natural light is a 12-sided, "spider web" patterned, domed skylight. The design and construction of the museum required more than 700 drawings and numerous sets of construction documents, as Wright battled with city authorities over building codes. A major problem was that city fire regulations required emergency exits on each floor. Technically, the Solomon R. Guggenheim Museum only has one floor! Wright's plans provided several spaces: in addition to the main gallery, there is a smaller adjoining circular structure originally housing administrative offices but now an exhibition space—the Monitor Building—a lower level auditorium which seats 300 people, and an annex which was completed in 1968 by Wes Peters.

Recognized by the American Institute of Architects as a structure representative of his contribution to American culture, the Solomon R. Guggenheim Museum opened shortly after Wright's death in 1959.

RIGHT: SOLOMON R. GUGGENHEIM MUSEUM (1956), New York, New York. Commissioned in 1943, it was to be 13 years before a suitable site was found for the museum and groundbreaking could begin. Throughout construction Wright battled with city officials whose building codes demanded fire exits on each floor. The problem with Wright's ziggurat design was that it was only one floor—a continuously flowing interior space. Outside, the cast concrete form is purely sculptural. Without any surface decorations the streamlined exterior sets the pattern for walls and spaces inside.

THE LEGACY

THE LEGACY

That Frank Lloyd Wright is highly regarded as one of the greatest architects of the 20th century is undeniable: he has left us with hundreds of completed works and thousands of pages of documents covering all of his years in practice as an architect. With a lifespan that extended nearly 100 years, Wright was witness to an age of change, the move into the machine age. It would be a period in which new architecture would emerge, but few displayed a greater creativity or inventiveness nor contributed more to its development than Frank Lloyd Wright.

Wright's importance to the history of architecture in general, and to American architecture in particular, in many ways rests on his introduction of the sophisticated method of composition—all rooms and spaces in his buildings were linked by means of a geometrical arrangement that differed from any other previously used by architects.

Wright was one of the first American architects to provide a viable alternative to the eclecticism in architecture that prevailed at the end of the 19th and the beginning of the 20th centuries. While many of his European contemporaries—Charles Rennie Mackintosh (1868–1928), Antonio Gaudi (1852–1926), or Victor Horta (1861–1947)—were generally working in the curvilinear or rectilinear modes of the Art Nouveau, Wright was building his first houses which destroyed the idea of the house as a large box containing a number of smaller boxes and was introducing the idea of interpenetrating and continuous space.

Rejecting the "traditional" approach, Wright extended the ideas of "organic architecture" derived from his mentor, Louis Sullivan, to include four important elements: spatial continuity, harmony with the environment, truth to materials and to structure, and the inter-relationship between all parts of the design. Organic architecture called for the design of interiors, furniture, and furnishings that were integral to the structures in which they were contained. In the preface to the English edition of the Wasmuth folio publication Wright wrote:

"In Organic Architecture then, it is quite impossible to consider the building as one thing, its furnishings another and its setting and environment still another. The Spirit in which these buildings are conceived sees all of these together at work as one thing. All are to be studiously foreseen and provided for in the nature of the structure. All these should become mere details of the character and completeness of the structure . . . The very chairs and tables, cabinets and even musical instruments . . . are of the building itself, never fixtures upon it . . ."

While not all these ideas were new, Wright's skill lay in his ability to blend them together into a philosophy and to find the expression of that philosophy in his designs.

With the designers of the Arts and Crafts Movement, the philosophy was rooted in ideas of tradition and had, in its architectural expression, a preoccupation with medievalism. Although sympathetic to their ideals, Wright's discriminating approach led him to refuse to contemplate the exclusion of the machine from the practice of design and his extensive use of "modern" materials—glass, steel, and concrete—enabled him to open up his houses and link them more closely with the landscape and their surroundings. The use of steel beams enabled him to span large expanses of space and to create dramatic cantilevered roofs. Without steel, Wright's ideas would not have been possible. In Unity Church, the box-like building of poured concrete with a reinforced slab roof was consistent with the properties of the building material. With this building, probably the first large public building to be built in this material, Wright also became the first architect of modern times to use an completely new imagery to describe the relationship between God and man.

Wright had a singular advantage over his European contemporaries in the fact that he was born in the United States. This gave him the opportunity first, to assimilate the great traditions of European art and architecture, second to be sceptical of those traditions when they were transplanted to the New World, and third, to reject them. He was no doubt aided in this by his own lack of *Beaux Arts* training which was the usual course for potential architects but also by the absence of any true "formal" training in architecture. Instead, there was a short spell in the School of Engineering at the University of Wisconsin under Allen D. Conover, the practical lessons learned on his uncle's farm in Spring Green—experiences which he later

said revealed to him an "underlying sense of the essential balance forces of nature"—and first-hand experience of Louis Sullivan's own philosophy, which reinforced his own views and which greatly influenced his own direction and growth.

Sullivan had argued for an architecture that enriched human life, architecture that would "characterize democracy." In searching for this architecture, Sullivan had established certain principles but was unable to evolve a technique that would realize the theory. Frank Lloyd Wright would be the architect to translate those ideas into buildings and also to transcend his mentor's aspirations. Dissatisfaction with the state of American society in the latter part of the 19th century and the belief that the anachronistic nature of buildings and cities were a major contributing factor to this state: Wright

sought to re-establish architecture as a creative tool for the enrichment of people's lives in America.

While he revered Sullivan's principles and his use of ornament, Wright nevertheless saw limitations to Sullivan's approach, the most significant of which was Sullivan's inability to see the importance of materials in architecture and his lack of spatial awareness. It was these two things, which were lacking in the master, that were to be developed in the student. They were to form the basis of Wright's theory of an organic architecture, in which spatial continuity and consistency was sought in the relationship of parts to the whole. Wright wanted the interiors of his buildings to be considered precisely in terms of their function and, as such, expressed on the exteriors, so that interior and exterior became one. He abandoned the

traditional construction technique of "post and lintel" in favour of continuous structure and he used materials according to their physical properties so that these alone dictated their use. By doing so Wright reversed the very principles of classical design which had governed architecture until then.

Wright can also be seen as more thoroughly American an architect than most of his predecessors and contemporaries in the sheer number of works and their wide geographical distribution: there are Frank Lloyd Wright buildings in more than 30 states—no

LEFT: THE ROBIE HOUSE (1906), Chicago, Illinois. The high-backed chairs are similar to earlier examples first designed for the 1899 Husser House and later used in the 1902 Ward Willits House. In some ways they are similar to chairs designed by the Scottish architect Charles Rennie Mackintosh. However, unlike Mackintosh's painted furniture with decorative inlay, Wright consistently used natural-finish oak surfaces.

RIGHT: TALIESIN WEST (1937), Scottsdale, Arizona. In 1937 Wright established an experimental desert camp that would serve as his winter home and studio until his death. Now the international headquarters of the Frank Lloyd Wright Foundation, Taliesin West is one of the 17 structures designed by Wright to be recognized by the American Institute of Architecture as representative of his contribution to American culture.

doubt there are close imitations of his works in all of them and, indeed, across the world. With the Wasmuth publication in Berlin in 1910 of Wright's works, his influence in Europe was to be seen: two concrete houses built by Robert van t'Hoff at Huis ter Heide between 1914 and 1916 reflect the influence of Wright. The leading Dutch architect and theorist H.P. Berlage (1856–1934) had also been pursuing the goal of an architecture that was truthful to materials and structure, and found in Wright's work the qualities he sought. Around 1906, a member of the so-called Prairie School of architects, W.G. Purcell, had introduced Berlage to the works of Sullivan and Wright. In 1911 Berlage visited the United States and saw Wright's Larkin Building—the central hall of which was to be the prototype of many similar halls in European office buildings after World War I—and many of the houses he had designed in and around Chicago. Back in Holland, Berlage lectured on what he had seen and wrote about it in the *Schweizer Bauzeitung* in 1912.

In Holland the name and the work of Frank Lloyd Wright became well known: J.J.P. Oud, who was at the forefront of the Dutch "De Stijl" movement, also regarded Wright highly and, in the first issue of the movement's art magazine (also called *De Stijl*), he emphasized the mechanistic content of his buildings, citing the Robie House as the building most developed along these mechanistic lines. In 1925 the official organ of the Amsterdam School of Architecture, the

magazine *Wendingen*, published no fewer than seven special issues devoted to Wright's life and works. The 1926 publication of a monograph of his work by H. de Fries spread knowledge of Wright further into Germany.

Meanwhile in the United States between 1925 and 1935 Wright turned his attention to writing and teaching, the results of which were to be seen in 1932 in the foundation of the Taliesin Fellowship which continues today at Taliesin West in Arizona as the Frank Lloyd Wright School of Architecture. Taliesin West is also the international headquarters of the Frank Lloyd Wright Foundation, which licenses Wright's designs, owns, and manages Taliesin at Spring Green in Wisconsin, runs Taliesin Architects (a profit-making subsidiary and successor to Wright's architecture and design

practice) and the Frank Lloyd Wright Archive, which contains more than 20,000 original drawings and more than 150,000 other documents, photographs, and items relating to Wright's life and works—works primarily from the second half of Wright's career since many of the earlier documents were lost in fires. In 1974, in Chicago, the Frank Lloyd Wright Home and Studio Foundation was established to acquire Wright's former home and restore it to its original 1909 design. Over 10,000 people a year visit the site.

Testament to Wright's fame, continuing importance, and popularity is the fact that, even after his death, his designs—primarily those genuinely planned by Wright but for one reason or another were never actually carried out—continue to be built.

Some owners of Wright buildings have returned to the original plans in order

ABOVE: THE HERMAN T. FASBENDER MEDICAL CLINIC (1957), Hastings, Minnesota. The enveloping structure of the roof—now re-roofed in copper according to Wright's original design—shelters the inhabitants from distracting views and noise from the street and provides a sense of privacy. The south side of the building, however, is largely of glass providing light-filled spaces and views onto private gardens.

ABOVE RIGHT: THE SETH PETERSON COTTAGE (1958), Reedsburg, Wisconsin. With views to the south, east, and west, the small cottage—only 880 square feet in area—opens up onto woods and across to Lake Delton. The cottage, now fully restored, offers the public the opportunity to live in a Wright house, even if it is only for a vacation.

to restore their properties: Mercedes-Benz Manhattan has occupied the Hoffman Auto Showroom at No. 430 Park Avenue in New York since 1957. In 1981 Mercedes-Benz hired Taliesin Architects to supervise a restoration which included the installation of the previously unexecuted design for a mirrored Mercedes-Benz insignia in the showroom's ceiling. In 1989 the owners of the

Meyers Medical Clinic in Dayton, Ohio constructed the built-in seating and plywood tables that Wright had designed for the waiting area in 1956; and in 1994 the new owners of the Herman T. Fasbender Medical Clinic in Hastings, Minnesota replaced the sheet metal roof and replaced it with a copper roof according to Wright's original specifications.

While most other architects' blueprints and plans lie rolled and forgotten—even during their lifetime—Wright, as usual, is the architect of exception and several of his designs have been completed since his death. For example, in 1957 Wright had been commissioned to design classroom, office, and laboratory space for Wichita State University's Teacher's College. Although pre-liminary plans were complete by 1958, funding delayed actual construction until 1963 and then only one of the two intended buildings was completed: the experimental elementary school was never built. The two, two-story, concrete and steel wings of the building—separated by an esplanade, reflect-ing pool, and a fountain—are supported by 200 pylons sunk deep into the unstable clay ground of the site. The exterior features large expanses of polished glass, red brick laid with matching mortar, and natural-colored aluminum-arched tracery. Inside the custom furniture and woodwork are of solid, red oak.

The untimely death of commissioner Seth Petersen in 1960 left his property in Reedsburg, Wisconsin unfinished and unoc-cupied. The 880-square foot cottage located

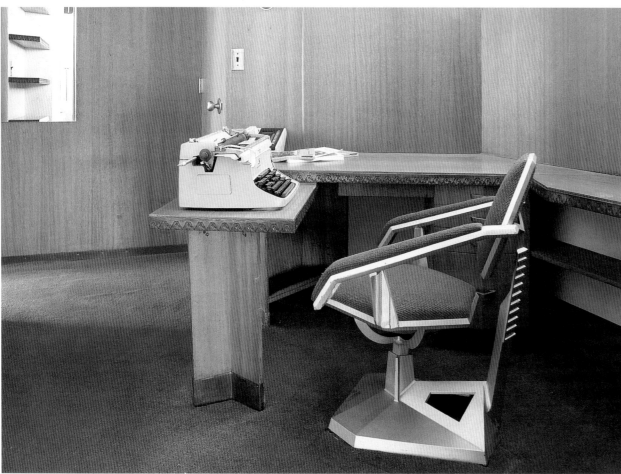

in Mirror Lake State Park in Wisconsin was sold, completed, and privately owned until 1966, when it was purchased by the state for park expansion and a period of prolonged neglect reduced it to near ruin. In 1989 an extensive restoration program returned the cottage to its former glory. Dividing the main living and dining area from the small kitchen is the central fireplace. Both the exterior and interior walls are of locally quarried sandstone and the floors are radiantly heated flagstones. Windows to the south, east, and west open up the small interior into the surrounding woodlands and provide a view over Mirror Lake. The furnishings inside the Seth Petersen Cottage were built from Wright's designs and include one of his famous long, built-in settees. Now available for vacation rentals, the Seth Petersen Cottage not only demonstrates Wright's skills at designing the most modest of living spaces, it also provides an opportunity for many people who could once only dream of living in a Wright house—even if for a short period!

An interesting Wright house "from beyond the grave" so to speak, is the Hilary and Joe Feldman House which was built in 1974. From the unbuilt projects, the Feldmans chose the plans for the Usonian House which Wright designed in 1939 for Lewis Bell for a site in west Los Angeles. Nevertheless, the Feldman House seems to fit perfectly in its site in a wooded section of Berkeley, California—despite the fact that Wright himself adopted a site-specific approach to design and that often design changes occurred during construction precisely because of the site. Furthermore, Wright was often working out variations on

ABOVE LEFT, TOP LEFT, AND LEFT: THE PRICE COMPANY TOWER (1952), BARTLESVILLE, OKLAHOMA. Interior views showing the detail of Wright's furnishings.

RIGHT: SOLOMON R. GUGGENHEIM MUSEUM (1956), New York, New York. A detail of the 12-sided, spider's web pattern of the domed skylight which covers the building and floods the interior with natural light.

the themes established in one particular house and developing them in other houses. Because his designs continuously evolved, it is not likely that Wright himself would have constructed a 1939 project at a much later date without changing and adapting it significantly. The Feldmans, however, have constructed their house exactly as it was originally planned.

Two further Wright designs which were unbuilt in his lifetime have added to his legacy. In 1971 the Director of Archives at the Frank Lloyd Wright Foundation, Bruce Brooks Pfeiffer, built a Wright-designed house in the grounds of Taliesin West at Scottsdale, Arizona. The single-story house, consisting of three loosely joined circular pavilions, varies from the original 1938 plans only in so far as the interior height has been increased and that it has been "transplanted" from its intended site in Palos Verdes, California where it was designed to be the home of Ralph Jester. The reason why the original Jester House was not built is largely because Wright designed it as an "All-Plywood" house. While plywood readily lends itself both to circular forms and to the climate of California, builders at the time were suspicious of the difficulties posed by "round buildings" and grossly overestimated the costs of construction. For the next 18 years Wright tried to convince no fewer than nine prospective clients as to the virtues of the design, but to no avail. Pfeiffer, himself a former Taliesin apprentice, assisted by his father, demonstrated that "Wright was Right."

The 1942 designs for the unexecuted Lloyd Burlingham House at El Paso in Texas has spawned not one, but two built houses—in Santa Fe, Texas and in Phoenix, Arizona. The original design was Wright's only foray into adobe construction and had been informally called "the pottery house." The plan of the house consists of two curved wings which wrap around a central patio to protect the inhabitants from the extreme heat of summer and the rough winds of winter in

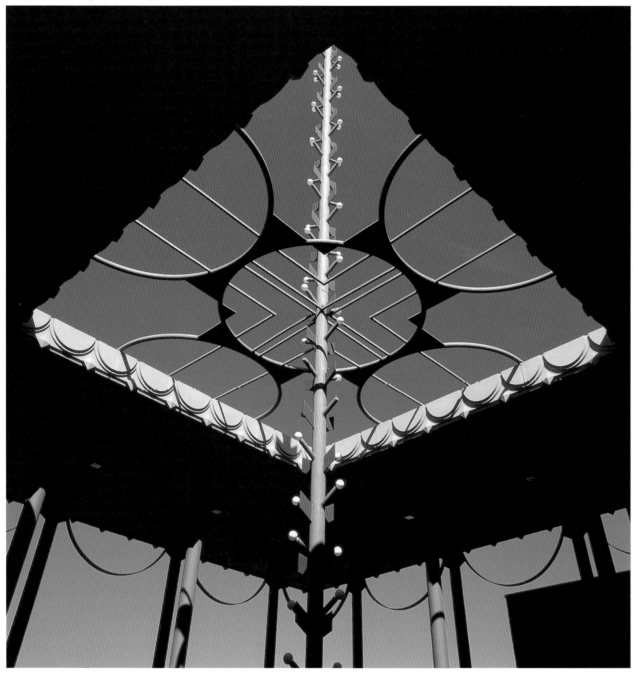

Texas. In charge of production on the Santa Fe site was Charles Montooth of Taliesin Associated Architects, while in Phoenix another T.A.A. architect, Charles Robert Schiffer, was supervising construction there. There was a slight problem in the fact that the owners of the Phoenix version believed that they were the sole beneficiaries of the design. However, it turns out that while the "finished" Burlingham plans are dated 1942, they belonged to a number of plans that Wright had been working on since 1929, so there were in fact, a number of versions planned for the original house, just as there are two versions of the built house today.

ABOVE AND RIGHT: THE JUVENILE CULTURAL STUDY CENTER (1958), Wichita State University, Kansas. Commissioned in 1957 to design classroom, laboratory, and office space for Wichita State University's College of Education, Wright's plans were not built until 1963 and then only one of the two buildings was completed—the Harry F. Corbin Educational Center. While continuing to explore technology and building materials—the concrete and steel structure is supported on 200 pylons sunk into the ground—Wright also continued to develop recurring design elements such as the arched aluminum traceries of the facings and the openings of the canopy through which the light tower extends. Similar light towers occur in the Annunciation Greek Orthodox Church.

Perhaps the greatest testament to the enduring power and achievement of Wright's architecture came in 1994 when the city of Madison, Wisconsin decided to build at a cost of $67 million a convention center that

THE LEGACY

utilized a design Wright first developed for the same site some 56 years earlier.

The plan for Monona Terrace began in 1938 as a city-county building with offices, courtroom, jail, and a railroad station. In the 1940s and 1950s the plans went through various developments and changes to re-emerge as a civic and cultural center, before finally encompassing an auditorium, exhibition hall, and community center. Despite Wright's obvious willingness constantly to alter plans to suit the commissioners, none of the projects was ever realized.

While the interiors of the buildings have been re-worked by Taliesin Architects in order to comply with contemporary city, fire, and safety regulations and in accordance with the building's new function, the exterior of the structure and its relationship to the

lakeside site are as Wright designed in 1959. The pre-cast concrete and steel building contains a 40,000-square foot exhibition hall, a 15,000-square foot ballroom and banqueting suite, a conference center with seating for over 300, meeting rooms, and a 68,000-square foot rooftop garden.

Inside, in the lobbies and pedestrian promenades, views of Lake Monona are framed by the arches of the facade, while outside a curving lakeside plaza supported on concrete pylons driven into the bed of the lake, carries pedestrians and cyclists onto the shoreline park beyond the building. On either side of the building, Wright's favorite three dimensional form, the spiral, is used in two ramps which lead to parking lots.

In Monona Terrace, due to open in fall 1997, Frank Lloyd Wright finally

OPPOSITE: THE DON AND VIRGINIA LOVENESS HOUSE (1955), Stillwater, Minnesota. The Lovenesses constructed their own home and made all the custom-designed furnishings. Wright's continuing development of Froebel-inspired geometric forms is evident in the concrete "sprites" (Far left), originally designed for the Midway Gardens in 1914, and in the furniture.

ABOVE: THE KALIL HOUSE (1955), Manchester, New Hampshire. An east coast location for a Wright building that draws on elements used in the California cast concrete houses of the 1920s.

FOLLOWING PAGE: THE ARIZONA BILTMORE HOTEL (1927), Phoenix, Arizona. This structure is now generally recognized as a collaboration between Wright and Albert Chase MacArthur, a former draftsman in the Oak Park Studio. While MacArthur's signature appears on the general plans, Wright provided the concrete-block system of construction. In 1973 fire destroyed the entire fourth floor and the copper roof: reconstruction and restoration using original drawings to reproduce the interiors was undertaken by Taliesin Architects.

achieved—if a little late—the public commission in his boyhood hometown that had eluded him in his lifetime.

APPENDICES

APPENDICES

1 Constructed works

1887 Hillside Home School, Building I,
Spring Green, Wisconsin (converted to
Taliesin Fellowship complex in 1933)

1886 Unity Chapel

1889 Frank Lloyd Wright House, Oak Park, Illinois

1890 Charnley House, Ocean Springs, Mississippi
Louis Sullivan House, Ocean Springs,
Mississippi

1891 Charnley House, Chicago, Illinois
Harlan House, Chicago, Illinois
MacHarg House, Chicago, Illinois

1892 Blossom House, Chicago, Illinois
(garage: 1907)
Clark House, LaGrange, Illinois
Emmond House, LaGrange, Illinois
Mrs. Thomas Gale House, Oak Park, Illinois
McArthur House, Chicago, Illinois
Parker House, Oak Park, Illinois
Albert Sulllivan House, Chicago, Illinois

1893 Lake Mendota Boathouse, Madison,
Wisconsin
Walter Gale House, Oak Park, Illinois
Peter Goan House, LaGrange, Illinois
Lamp Cottage, Lake Mendota, Madison,
Wisconsin
Frank Lloyd Wright House, Oak Park, Illinois:
playroom addition

1894 Winslow House, River Forest, Illinois
Bagley House, Hillsdale, Illinois
Basset House, Oak Park, Illinois: remodeling
Roloson Apartments, Chicago, Illinois

1895 Francis Apartments, Chicago, Illinois

Francisco Terrace Apartments, Chicago,
Illinois
Moore House, Oak Park, Illinois
(rebuilt after fire: 1923)
Waller Apartments, Chicago, Illinois
Williams House, River Forest, Illinois

1896 Goodrich House, Oak Park, Illinois
Heller House, Chicago, Illinois
Romeo and Juliet Windmill Tower, Hillside
Home School, Spring Green, Wisconsin

1897 Frank Lloyd Wright House, Oak Park, Illinois:
studio addition
George Furbeck House, Oak Park, Illinois
Wallis Boathouse, Lake Delavan, Illinois

1898 Rollin Furbeck House, Oak Park, Illinois
River Forest Golf Club, Illinois
(additions: 1901)
Smith House, Oak Park, Illinois
Waller House, River Forest, Illinois (gate
house and gardener's cottage: 1901)

1899 Husser House, Chicago, Illinois

1900 Jesse Adams House, Longwood, Illinois
William Adams House, Chicago, Illinois
Bradley House, Kankakee, Illinois
Foster House, Chicago, Illinois
Goodsmith House, Lake Delavan, Wisconsin
Hickox House, Kankakee, Illinois
Pitkin Lodge, Desbarats, Ontario, Canada
Wallis House, Lake Delavan, Wisconsin (gate
house remodeled: 1901)

1901 Davenport House, River Forest, Illinois
Henderson House, Elmhurst, Illinois
Jones House, Boathouse and Gate Lodge,
Lake Delavan, Wisconsin
Thomas House, Oak Park, Illinois

1902 Dana House, Springfirld, Illinois
Fricke House, Highland Park, Illinois
George Gerts House, Whitehall, Michigan

Walter Gerts House, Whitehall, Michigan
Heurtley House, Oak Park, Illinois
Hillside Home Building II, Spring Green,
Wisconsin
Francis Little House II, Peoria, Illinois
Ross House, Lake Delavan, Wisconsin
Spencer House, Lake Delavan, Wisconsin
Willits House, Highland Park, Illinois

1903 Abraham Lincoln Center, Chicago, Illinois
Barton House, Buffalo, New York
Cheney House, Oak Park, Illinois
Freeman House, Hillsdale, Illinois
Larkin Building, Buffalo, New York
Martin House, Oak Park, Illinois
Scoville Park Fountain, Oak Park, Illinois
Walser House, Chicago, Illinois

1904 Lamp House II, Madison, Wisconsin
Martin House and Conservatory, Buffalo,
New York
Unity Temple, Oak Park, Illinois

1905 Adams House, Highland Park, Illinois
Baldwin House II, Kenilworth, Illinois
Bank Building II, Dwight, Illinois
Brown House, Evanston, Illinois
E-Z Polish Factory, Chicago, Illinois
Gilpin House, Oak Park, Illinois
Glasner House, Glencoe, Illinois
Hardy House, Racine, Wisconsin
Heath House, Buffalo, New York
Johnson House, Lake Delavan, Wisconsin
Lawrence Memorial Library (interior),
Springfield, Illinois
Rookery Building entrance, lobbies, and
balcony-court remodeling, Chicago,
Illinois

1906 Beachy House, Oak Park, Illinois
De Rhodes House, South Bend, Indiana
Fuller House, Glencoe, Illinois
Gridley House, Batavia, Illinois

Hoyt House, Geneva, Illinois
Millard House, Highland Park, Illinois
Nicholas House, Flossmoor, Illinois
River Forest Tennis Club, Illinois
Robie House, Chicago, Illinois

1907 Cummings Real Estate Office, River Forest,
        Illinois
     Remodeling of Fabyan House, Geneva,
        Illinois
     Remodeling of Fox River Country Club,
        Geneva, Illinois
     Hunt House, La Grange, Illinois
     Larkin Company Pavilion for Jamestown
        Exposition, Virginia
     Pebbles and Balch Shop, Oak Park, Illinois
     Jane Porter House ("Tanyderi"), Spring
        Green, Wisconsin
     Sutton House, McCook, Nebraska
     Tomek House, Riverside, Illinois
     Westcott House, Springfield, Ohio

1908 Avery Coonley House, Riverside, Illinois
        (gardener's cottage: 1911; playhouse: 1912)
     Browne's Bookstore, Chicago, Illinois
     Davidson House, Buffalo, New York
     Evans House, Chicago, Illinois
     Gilmore House, Madison, Wisconsin
     Horner House, Chicago, Illinois
     Francis Little House, Wayzata, Minnesota
     May House, Grand Rapids, Michigan
     Roberts House, River Forest, Illinois
     Stockman House, Mason City, Iowa

1909 Arcade Building, Chicago, Illinois
     Gale House, Oak Park, Illinois
     Baker House II, Wilmette, Illinois
     City National Bank and Hotel, Mason City,
        Iowa
     Ingalls House, River Forest, Illinois
     Steffans House, Chicago, Illinois
     George C. Stewart House, Montecito,
        California
     Thurber Art Gallery, Chicago, Illinois
     Ziegler House, Frankfort, Kentucky

1910 Amberg House, Grand Rapids, Michigan
     Como Orchard Summer Colony (partly built),
        Darby, Montana
     Irving House, Decatur, Illinois

Universal Portland Cement Company Exhibit,
   Madison Square Garden, New York

1911 American System Ready-Cut Houses
        (prototypes) for Richards Company,
        Milwaukee, Wisconsin
     Angster House, Lake Bluff, Illinois
     Balch House, Oak Park, Illinois
     Pavilion, Banff National Park, Alberta,
        Canada
     Booth House, Glencoe, Illlinois
     Lake Geneva Inn, Wisconsin
     Taliesin, Spring Green, Wisconsin
        (living quarters destroyed by fire in
        1914)

1912 Greene House, Aurora, Illinois

1913 Adams House II, Oak Park, Illinois,
     Francis Little House II, Wayzata, Minnesota

1914 Midway Gardens, Chicago, Illinois
        (demolished)
     Taliesin II, Spring Green, Wisconsin (original
        studios and worshops survive second
        fire, 1925. Rebuilt living quarters
        destroyed again)

1915 Allen House, Wichita, Kansas
     Bach House, Chicago, Illinois
     Brigham House, Glencoe, Illinois
     A.D. German Warehouse, Richland Center,
        Wisconsin
     Ravine Bluffs Housing Development,
        Glencoe, Illinois

1916 Bagley House, Grand Beach, Michigan
     Aline Barnsdall House ("Hollyhock House"),
        Los Angeles, California
     Bock House, Milwaukee, Wisconsin
     Carr House, Grand Beach, Michigan
     Duplex apartments for Minkwitz Ready-Cut
        Systems, Milwaukee, Wisconsin
     Vosburgh House, Grand Beach, Michigan

1917 Hunt House, Oshkosh, Wisconsin
     Hayashi House, Tokyo, Japan

1918 Fukuhara House, Hakone, Japan
     Yamamura House, Ashiya, Japan

1921 Mrs. Thomas Gale House, Whitehall,
        Michigan
     Giuy Gakuen School of the Free Spirit,
        Tokyo, Japan

1922 Imperial Hotel, Tokyo, Japan
     Barnsdall Kindergarten ("Little Dipper"),
        Los Angeles, California
     Freeman House, Los Angeles, California
     Lowe House, Eagle Rock, California

1923 Ennis House, Los Angeles, California
     Alice Millard House ("La Miniatura")
        Pasadena, California
     Storer House, Los Angeles, California

1924 Indian Figure Sculptures (Nakoma and
        Nakomis), Madison, Wisconsin. Placed
        in courtyard of S.C. Johnson Wax
        Company Research Tower.

1925 Taliesin III, Spring Green, Wisconsin
        (rebuilding of living quarters)

1927 Arizona Biltmore Hotel, Phoenix, Arizona
        (with Albert McArthur)
     Martin House, Derby, New York

1928 Ocatillo, Chandler, Arizona (Wright's
        temporary southwestern headquarters)

1929 Jones House II, Tulsa, Oklahoma

1933 Taliesin Fellowship complex, Spring Green,
        Wisconsin: additions to existing Hillside
        Home School. Partly built theater
        destroyed by fire in 1952

1934 Willey House, Minneapolis, Minnesota

1935 Kaufmann House ("Fallingwater") Bear Run,
        Pennsylvania (Guest house: 1938)

1936 Hanna House ("Honeycomb House"), Palo
        Alto, California
     Jacobs House, Westmoreland, Wisconsin
     S.C. Johnson Wax Company Administration
        Building, Racine, Wisconsin
     Roberts House, Marquette, Michigan

1937 Johnson House ("Wingspread"), Racine,
        Wisconsin
        Edgar J. Kaufmann Sr. Offices, Pittsburgh

1938 Bazett House, Hillsborough, California
        Florida Southern College, Lakeland, Florida
            (construction through 1959)
        Midway Farm Buildings, Spring Green,
            Wisconsin
        Rebhohn House, Great Neck, Long Island,
            New York
        Taliesin West, Scottsdale, Arizona (Wright's
            winter headquarters)

1939 Armstrong House, Gary, Indiana
        Goetsch-Winkler House I, Okemos, Michigan
        Rosenbaum House, Florence, Alabama
        Sturges House ("Skyeway"), Brentwood
            Heights, California
        Suntop Homes (quadruple house), Ardmore,
            Pennsylvania

1940 Auldbrass Plantation, Yemassee, South
            Carolina
        Baird House, Amherst, Massachusetts
        Christie House, Bernardsville, New Jersey
        Community Church, Kansas City, Missouri
        Euchtman House, Baltimore, Maryland
        Lewis House, Libertyville, Illinois
        Manson House, Wausau, Wisconsin
        Oboler Gatehouse, Los Angeles,
            California
        Pauson House, Phoenix, Arizona
        Pew House, Madison, Wisconsin
        Pope House, Falls Church, Virginia
        Sondern House, Kansas City, Missouri

1941 Affleck House, Bloomfield Hills, Michigan
        Griggs Gouse, Tacoma, Washington
        Oboler Gatehouse and Retreat, Los Angeles,
            California
        Richardson House, Glenridge, New Jersey
        Wall House ("Snowflake"), Plymouth,
            Michigan

1942 Jacobs House (Solar Hemicycle), Middleton,
            Wisconsin

1944 S.C. Johnson Wax Company Research Tower,
            Racine, Wisconsin

1945 Friedman House, Pecos, New Mexico
        Grant House, Cedar Rapids, Iowa
        Taliesin Dams, Spring Green, Wisconsin

1946 Brauner House, Okemos, Michigan
        Walter House and River Pavilion,
            Quasqueton, Iowa

1947 Alpauch House, Northport, Michigan
        Bullbullian House, Rochester, Minnesota
        Keys House, Rochester, Minnesota
        Lamberson House, Oskaloosa, Iowa
        First Unitarian Society Meeting House,
            Madison, Wisconsin
        Master plans for Galesburg Village Dwellings
            and Parkwyn Village Dwellings,
            Kalamazoo, Michigan and Usonia
            Homes, Pleasantville, New York

1948 Adelman House, Fox Point, Wisconsin
        Alsop House, Oskaloosa, Iowa
        Anthony House, Benton Harbor, Michigan
        Buehler House, Orinda, California
        Eppstein House, Galesburg Village,
            Kalamazoo, Michigan
        Hughes House ("Fountainhead"), Jackson,
            Mississippi
        Laurent House, Rockford, Illinois
        Levin House, Parkwyn Village, Kalamazoo,
            Michigan
        Smith House, Bloomfield Hills, Michigan
        V.C. Morris Gift Shop, San Francisco,
            California
        Walker House, Carmel, California
        Welziemer House, Oberlin, Ohio

1949 Cabaret-Theater, Taliesin West, Scottsdale,
            Arizona
        Edwards House, Okemos, Michigan
        Friedman House, Usonia Homes,
            Pleasantville, New York
        Sterlin House, Usonia Homes, Pleasantville,
            New York
        McCartney House, Parkwyn Village,
            Kalamazoo, Michigan
        Weisblatt House, Galesburg Village,
            Kalamazoo, Michigan

1950 Anderton Court Center, Beverly Hills,
            California

Berger House, San Anselmo, California
Brown House, Parkwyn Village, Kalamazoo,
    Michigan
Carr House, Glenview, Illinois
Carlson House, Phoenix, Arizona
David House, Marion, Indiana
Gillin House, Dallas, Texas
Harper House, St. Joseph, Michigan
Matthews House, Atherton, California
Meyer House, Galesburg Village, Kalamazoo,
    Michigan
Miller House, Charles City, Iowa
Muirhead House, Plato Center, Illinois
Neils House, Minneapolis, Minnesota
O'Donnell House, East Lansing, Michigan
Palmer House, Ann Arbor, Michigan
Schaberg House, Okemos, Michigan
Shavin House, Chatanooga, Tennessee
Smith Houes, Jefferson, Wisconsin
Sweeton House, Merchantville, New Jersey
Winn House, Parkwyn Village, Kalamazoo,
    Michigan
Wright House, Phoenix, Arizona
Zimmerman House, Manchester, New
    Hampshire

1950 First Christian Church, Phoenix, Arizona

1951 Adelman House (Usonian Automatic),
            Phoenix, Arizona
        Austin House, Greenville, South Carolina
        Chadroudi House II, Lake Mahopac,
            New York
        Elam House, Austin, Minnesota
        Fuller House, Pass Christian, Mississippi
        Globe House, Lake Forest, Illinois
        Kinney House, Lancaster, Wisconsin
        Kraus House, Kirkwood, Missouri
        Pearce House, Monrovia, California
        Reisley House, Usonia Homes, Pleasantville,
            New York
        Rubin House, Canton, Ohio
        Staley House, Madison, Wisconsin

1952 Blair House, Cody, Wyoming
        Brandes House, Bellevue, Washington
        Goddard House, Plymouth, Michigan
        Hillside Playhouse redesign and rebuilding,
            Spring Green, Wisconsin
        Hillside Theater, Spring Green, Wisconsin

Lewis House, Tallahassee, Florida
Lindholm House, Cloquet, Minnesota
Marden House, McLean, Virginia
Pieper House, Paradise Valley, Arizona
Price Tower office and apartment building,
    Bartlesville, Oklahoma
Teater House, Bliss, Idaho

1953 Bommer Cottage, Phoneix, Arizona
    Dobkins House, Canton, Ohio
    Penfield House I, Willoughby, Ohio
    Riverview Terrace restuarant, Spring Green,
        Wisconsin
    Sander House, Stamford, Connecticut
    Robert Llewellyn Wright House, Silver
        Springs, Maryland
    Usonian Exhibition House pavilion,
        New York, New York

1954 Bachman-Wilson House, Millstone,
        New Jersey
    Beth Sholom Synagogue, Elkins Park,
        Pennsylvania
    Boulter House, Cincinnati, Ohio
    Christian House, Lafayette, Indiana
    Clark-Arnold House, Columbus, Wisconsin
    Fawcett House, Los Banos, California
    Feiman House, Canton, Ohio
    Frederick House, Barrington, Illinois
    Greenberg House, Dousman, Wisconsin
    Hagan House, Uniontown, Pennsylvania
    Keland House, Racine, Wisconsin
    Price House, Bartlesville, Oklahoma
    Price House, Phoenix, Arizona
    Thaxton House, Houston, Texas

1955 Dallas (Kalita Humphreys) Theater Center
    Hoffman House III, Manursing Island, Rye,
        New York
    Kalil House, Manchester, New Hampshire
    Loveness House, Stillwater, Minnesota
    Pappas House, St. Louis County, Mississippi
    Rayward House, New Canaan, Connecticut
    Sunday House, Marshaltown, Iowa
    Tonkens House, Cincinnati, Ohio
    Turkel House, Detroit, Michigan

1956 Annunciation Greek Orthodox Church,
        Milwaukee, Wisconsin

Hoffman Auto Showroom, New York, New
    Yoek
Bott House, Kansas City, Missouri
Friedman House, Deerfield, Illinois
Solomon R. Guggenheim Museum,
    New York, New York
Kundert Clinic, San Louis Obispo, California
Meyer Clinic, Dayton, Ohio
Music Pavilion, Taliesin West, Scottsdale,
    Arizona
Nooker House (Lloyd Wright Studio)
    restoration, Oak Park, Illinois
Pre-Fab I for Marshall Erdman Associates,
    Madison, Wisconsin
Smith House, Kane County, Illinois
Spencer House, Brandywine Head, Delaware
Stromquist House, Bountiful, Utah
Walton House, Modesto, California

1957 Boswell House II, Cincinnati, Ohio
    Fasbender Clinic, Hastings, Minnesota
    Gordon House, Aurora, Oregon
    Kinney House, Amarillo, Texas
    Lindholm Service Station, Cloquet, Minnesota
    Marin County Civic Center, San Rafael,
        California (construction through 1966)
    Pre-Fab II for Marshall Erdman Associates,
        Madison, Wisconsin
    Schulz House, St. Joseph, Michigan
    Trier House, Des Moines, Iowa
    Duey Wright House, Wausau, Wisconsin
    Wyoming Valley School, Wisconsin

1958 Ablin House, Bakersfield, California
    Juvenile Cultural Study Center Building A,
        University of Wichita, Kansas
    Lockridge, McIntyre and Whalen Clinic,
        Whitefish, Montana
    Olfelt House, St. Louis Park, Minnesota
    Petersen Cottage, Lake Delton, Wisconsin
    Pilgrim Congregational Church, Redding,
        California (partly built)

1959 Grady Gammage Memorial Auditorium,
        Arizona State University, Tempe,
        Arizona

2 Projects

1885 University Avenue Power House, Madison,
        Wisconsin

1887 Misses Lloyd Jones House, Spring Green,
        Wisconsin

1890 Cooper House, La Grange, Illinois

1893 Lake Monona Boathouse, Madison,
        Wisconsin
    Library and Museum, Milwaukee, Wisconsin
        (competition project)

1894 Concrete Monolithic Bank
    Orris Goan House, LaGrange, Illinois
    McAfee House, Chicago, Illinois

1895 Amusement Park, Wolf Lake, Illinois
    Baldwin House, Oak Park, Illionois
    Lexington Terrace Apartment Building,
        Chicago, Illinois
    Luxfer Prism Company Skyscraper, Chicago,
        Illinois

1896 Devin House, Chicago, Illinois
    Perkins Apartment, Chicago, Illinois
    Roberts Houses (four houses), Ridgeland,
        Illinois

1897 All Souls Building, Lincoln Center, Chicago
    Chicago Screw Company Factory Building,
        Chicago, Illinois

1898 Mozart Gardens restaurant remodeling,
        Chicago, Illinois

1899 Cheltenham Beach Resort, nr. Chicago,
        Illinois
    Eckhart House, River Forest, Illinois

1900 Abraham Lincoln Center, Chicago, Illinois
    Francis W. Little House I, Peoria, Illinois
    Motion Picture Theater, Los Angeles,
        California
    School, Crosbytown, Texas

1902 Lake Delavan Yacht Club, Wisconsin
    Metzger House, Ontario, Canada

Waller House I, Charlevoix, Michigan
Yahara Boat Club, Madison, Wisconsin

1903 Chicago and Northwestern Railway: stations
for Chicago suburbs, Chicago, Illinois
Lamp House I, Madison, Wisconsin
Roberts Quadruple Block Plan (24 houses),
Oak Park, Illinois
Waller House II, Charlevoix, Michigan
Frank Lloyd Wright Studio-House, Oak Park,
Illinois

1904 Baldwin House I, Kenilworth, Illinois
Bank Building I, Dwight, Illinois
Clarke House, Peoria, Illinois
House in Highland Park, Illinois
Scudder House, Desbarats, Ontario, Canada
Ullman House, Oak Park, Illinois
Larkin Company Workmen's Rowhouses,
Buffalo, New York

1905 Barnes House, McCook, Nebraska
"House on a Lake"
"Varnish Factory"
Concrete Apartment Building, Chicago,
Illinois
Moore House pergola and pavilion,
Oak Park, Illinois

1906 Bock Studio-House, Maywood, Illinois
Devin House, Eliot, Maine
Gerts House, Glencoe, Illinois
Ludington House, Dwight, Illinois
Shaw House, Montreal, Canada
Stone House, Glencoe, Illinois

1907 McCormick House, Lake Forest, Illinois
Municipal Art Gallery, Chicago, Illinois
Porter House II, Spring Green, Wisconsin

1908 Guthrie House, Sewanee, Tennessee
Horseshoe Inn, Estes Park, Colorado
Melson House, Mason City, Iowa

1909 Brown House, Geneva, Illinois
"City Dwelling with Glass Front"
Larwell House, Muskegon, Michigan
Lexington Terrace (second project), Chicago,
Illinois
Roberts House, River Forest, Illinois

Town Hall, Glencoe, Illinois
Town of Bitter Root, Darby, Montana
Waller House: bathing pavilion, Charlevoix,
Michigan
Waller Rental Houses (three-house scheme)

1910 Frank Lloyd Wright House-Studio,
Viale Verdi, Fiesole, Italy

1911 Adams House I, Oak Park, Illinois
Christian Catholic Church, Zion, Illinois
Coonley House, Riverside, Illinois:
greenhouse and kindergarten
Cutten House, Downer's Grove, Illinois
Ebenshade House, Milwaukee, Wisconsin
Heath House, Buffalo, New York: garage and
stables
Madison Hotel, Madison, Wisconsin
North Shore Electric Tram waiting stations for
the Chicago suburbs, Chicago, Illinois
Porter House III, Spring Green, Wisconsin
Schroeder House, Wilwaukee, Wisconsin

1912 Dress Shop, Oak Park, Illinois
Florida House, Palm Beach, Florida
Kehl Dance Academy House and Shops,
Madison, Wisconsin
San Francisco Call newspaper building,
San Francisco, California
Schoolhouse, LaGrange, Illinois
Taliesin Cottages (two buildings),
Spring Green, Wisconsin

1913 Block of City Row Houses, Chicago, Illinois
Carnegie Library, Ottowa, Ontario, Canada
Hilly House, Brookfield, Illinois
Kellog House, Milwaukee, Wisconsin
Mendelson House, Albany, New York

1914 Concert Gardens, Chicago, Illinois
State Bank, Spring Green, Wisconsin
United States Embassy building, Tokyo,
Japan
Vogelsang Dinner Gardens, Chicago,
Illinois

1915 Chinese Restaurant, Milwaukee, Wisconsin
Model Quarter Section Development,
Chicago, Illinois
Wood House, Decateur, Illinois

1916 Behn House, Grand Beach, Michigan
Converse House, Palisades Park, Michigan

1917 Odawara Hotel, Nagoya, Japan
Powell House, Wichita, Kansas

1918 Count Immu House, Tokyo, Japan
Viscount Inouge House, Tokyo, Japan
Motion picture theater, Tokyo, Japan

1919 Japanese Print Gallery for the Spaulding
Collection, Boston, Massachusetts
"Monolith Homes," Racine, Wisconsin

1920 Barnsdall House A and B, Los Angeles,
California
"Cantilevered Steel Skyscraper"
Apartments, theater and shops, Olive Hills,
Los Angeles

1921 Doheney Ranch Development, near
Los Angeles, California
"Glass and Copper Skyscraper"
Baron Goto House, Tokyo, Japan
Block House, Los Angeles, California

1922 Johnson Desert Compound and Shrine,
Death Valley, California
Merchandising Building, Los Angeles,
California
Desert Springs House, Mojave Desert,
California
Tahoe Summer Colony, Lake Tahoe,
California

1923 Martin House, Buffalo, New York

1924 Gladney House, Fort Worth, Texas
Nakoma Country Club, Madison,
Wisconsin
National Life Insurance Company Skyscraper,
Chicago, Illinois
Planetarium, Sugar Loaf Mountain,
Maryland

1925 Millard Gallery, Pasadena, California
Phi Gamma Delta Fraternity House,
University of Wisconsin, Madison,
Wisconsin
"Steel Cathedral," New York

1926 Kinder Symphony Playhouse, Oak Park,
    Illinois
    Standardised Concrete and Copper Gas
        Station

1928 Beach Cottages, Ras-El-Bar Island, Damiette,
        Egypt
    Blue Sky Burial Terraces, Buffalo, New York
    Cudney House, Chandler, Arizona
    Jones House I, Tulsa, Oklahoma
    Low-cost concrete block houses, Chandler,
        Arizona
    San Marcos in the Desert Resort Hotel,
        Chandler, Arizona
    San Marcos Water Gardens, Chandler,
        Arizona
    School, La Jolla, California
    Young House, Chandler, Arizona

1929 St. Mark's Tower, New York

1930 Automobile with catilevered top
    Cabins for desert or woods, YMCA, Chicago,
        Illinois
    Grouped apartment towers, Chicago, Illinois
    Noble Apartment House, Los Angeles,
        California

1931 *The Capital Journal* Newspaper Building,
        Salem, Oregon
    "House on the Mesa," Denver, Colorado
    Three schemes for "A Century of Progress,"
        World's Fair, Chicago, Illinois

1932 Automobile and airplane filling and service
        station
    Movie House and shops, Michigan City,
        Indiana
    Pre-fabricated sheet steel farm units
    Highway overpass
    New theater
    Overhead filling station
    Pre-fabricated sheet steel and glass roadside
        markets
    Willey House I, Minneapolis, Minnesota

1934 Broadacre City model and exhibition plans
    Willey House II
    Helicopter project
    Road machine project

Train project
"Zoned House Number 1"

1935 Hoult House, Wichita, Kansas
    Lusk House, Huron, South Dakota
    Marcus House, Dallas, Texas
    "Zoned City House"
    "Zoned Country House"
    "Zoned Suburban House"

1936 Little San Marcos in the Desert Resort Inn,
        Chandler, Arizona

1937 100 All Steel Houses, Los Angeles,
        California
    Borglum Studio, Black Hills, South Dakota
    Bramson Dress Shop, Oak Park, Illinois
    "Memorial to the Soil" chapel, Southern
        Wisconsin
    Garage for Parker House, Janesville,
        Wisconsin

1938 Jester All-Plywood Houses, Palos Verde,
        California (design constructed by Bruce
        Brooks Pfeiffer, Director of Archives at
        the Frank Lloyd Wright Foundation, in
        the grounds of Taliesin West, Scottsdale,
        Arizona, 1971)
    Johnson Gatehouse and Farm Group,
        Wind Point, Wisconsin
    Jargensen House, Evanston, Illinois
    McCallum House, Northampton,
        Massachusetts
    Monona Terrace, Madison Civic Center,
        Wisconsin (building commenced in
        1994 based on revised plans from 1959.
        Opening planned for late 1997)
    Smith House (Pine Tree) Piedmont Pines,
        California

1939 Bell House, Los Angeles, California
        (project built in 1974 as Feldman House
        in Berkeley, California)
    Carlson House, Superior, Wisconsin
    Crystal Heights Hotel, Shops and Theaters,
        Washington D.C.
    Front gates for Taliesin, Spring Green,
        Wisconsin
    Mauer House, Los Angeles, California
    Spivey House, Fort Lauderdale, Florida

Usonian House Development
    (seven buildings), Okemos, Michigan

1940 Model House (exhibition project)
        Museum of Modern Art, New York
    Nesbitt House, Carmel Bay, California
    Oboler House ("Eaglefeather"), Los Angeles,
        California
    Pence House, Hilo, Hawaii
    Rentz House, Madison, Wisconsin
    Watkins Studio, Barnegate City, New Jersey
    Methodist Church, Spring Green,
        Wisconsin

1941 Barton House, Pine Bluff, Wisconsin
    Dayer Music Studio, Detroit, Michigan
    Ellinwood House, Deerfield, Illinois
    Field House, Peru, Illinois
    Guenther House ("Mountain Lakes"),
        East Caldwell, New Jersey
    Petersen House, West Racine, Wisconsin
    Schevill House, Tuscon, Arizona
    Sigma Chi Fraternity House, Hanover,
        Indiana
    Sundt House, Madison, Wisconsin
    Waterstreet Studio, nr. Spring Green,
        Wisconsin

1942 Jacobs House (Solar Hemicycle), Middleton,
        Wisconsin
    Burlingham House, El Paso, Texas (two
        versions of the planned house were
        built in the 1980s: one in Santa Fe,
        New Mexico, the second in Phoenix,
        Arizona.)
    Circle Pines Center, Cloverdale, Wisconsin
    Cloverleaf Quadruple Housing, Pittsfield,
        Massachusetts
    Cooperative Homesteads: Housing for Detroit
        Auto Workers, Michigan

1943 Hein House, Chippewa Falls, Wisconsin
    McDonald House, Washington, D.C
    Richardson Restaurant and Service Station,
        Spring Green, Wisconsin

1944 Loeb House (Pergola House), Redding,
        Connecticut
    Harlan House, Omaha, Nebraska
    Wells House, Minneapolis, Minnesota

1945 Adelman Laundry, Milwaukee, Wisconsin
Berdan House, Ludington, Michigan
Elizabeth Arden Desrt Spa, Phoenix, Arizona
"Glass House" project for *Ladies' Home Journal*
Haldorn House (The Wave) Carmel, California
Slater House, Rhode Island
Stamm House, Lake Delavan, Wisconsin

1946 President's House, Olivet College, Michigan
Dayer House and Music pavilion, Bloomfield Hills, Michigan
Garrison House, Lansing, Michigan
Hause House, Lansing, Michigan
Housing for State Teacher's College, Lansing, Michigan
Morris House I, San Francisco, California
Munroe House, Knox County, Ohio
Newman House, Lansing Michigan
Oboler Studio, Los Angeles, California
Panshin House, State Teacher's College, Lansing, Michigan
Pinderton House, Cambridge, Massachusetts
Pinkerton House, Fairfax County, Virginia
Rogers Lacy Hotel, Dallas, Texas
Sarabhi Administration Building and Store, Ahmedabad, India
Van Dusen House, Lansing, Michigan

1947 Wetmore Auto Display Room and Workshop, Detroit, Michigan
Bell House, East St. Louis, Illinois
Black House, Rochester, Minnesota
Boomer House, Phoenix, Arizona
Butterfly Bridge over the Wisconsin River, Spring Green, Wisconsin
Cottage Group Resort Hotel, Los Angeles, California
San Antonio Transit Company Depot, San Antonio, Texas
Daphne Funeral Chapels, San Francisco, California
Hamilton House, Brookline, Vermont
Hartford House, Hollywood, California
Houston House, Schuyler County, Illinois
Keith House, Oakland County, Michigan
Marting House, Northampton, Ohio
Palmer House, Phoenix, Arizona
Pike House, Los Angles, California

Ayn Rand House, near Redding, Connecticut
Sports Club, Hollywood, California
Wheeler House, Hinsdale, Illinois
Wilkie House, Hennepin County, Minnesota
Valley National Bank, Tuscon, Arizona

1948 Barney Cottage, Spring Green, Wisconsin
Bergman House, St. Petersburg, Florida
Bimson Penthouse, Phoenix, Arizona
Crater Resort, Meteor Crater, Arizona
Daphne House, San Francisco, California
Ellison House, Bridgewater Township, New Jersey
Feenberg House, Fox Point, Wisconsin
Hageman House, Peoria, Illinois
Margolis House, Kalamazoo, Michigan
McCord House, North Arlington, New Jersey
Miller House, Pleasantville, New York
Muehlberger House, East Lansing, Michigan
Scully House, Woodbridge, Connecticut
Valley National Bank and Shopping Center, Sunnyslope, Arizona

1949 Bloomfield House, Tuscon, Arizona
Dabney House, Chicago, Illinois
Drummond House, Santa Fe, New Mexico
Goetsch-Winkler House II, Okemos, Michigan
John House, Oconomowoc, Wisconsin
Lea House, Ashville, North Carolina
Publicker House, Haverford, Pennsylvania
San Francisco Bay Bridge: Southern Crossing
Kauffman Self Service Garage, Pittsburgh
Theater for the New Theater Corp., Hartford, Connecticut
Windforhr House, Fort Worth, Texas
YMCA Building, Racine, Wisconsin

1950 Achuff House, Wauwatosa, Wisconsin
Auerbach House, Pleasantville, New York
Carroll House, Wauwatosa, Wisconsin
Chahroudi House I, Lake Mahopac, New York
Conklin House, New Ulm, Minnesota
Grover House, Syracuse, New York
Hargrove House, Berkeley, California
Jackson House, Madison, Wisconsin
Jacobsen House, Montreal, Canada
Montooth House, Rushville, Illinois
Sabin House, Battle Creek, Michigan

Leon Small House, West Orange, New Jersey
Southwestern Christian Seminary, Phoenix, Arizona (Construction of First Christian Church began 1970 and completed 1972)
Stevens House, Park Ridge, Illinois
Strong House, Kalamazoo, Michigan
Wassel House, Philadelphia

1951 Clarke Cottage, Carmel, California
Hall House, Ann Arbor, Michigan
Haynes House, Fort Wayne, Indiana
Kauffman House ("Boulder House"), Palm Springs, California
Schevill Studio, Tucson, Arizona

1952 Affleck House II, Bloomfield Hills, Michigan
Bailleres House, Acapulco, Mexico
Clifton House, Oakland, New Jersey
Cooke House, Virginia Beach, Virginia
Leesburg Floating Gardens, Florida
Paradise on Wheels Trailer Park, Paradise Valley, Arizona
Sturtevant House, Oakland, California
Swann House, near Detroit, Michigan
Wainer House, Valdosta, Georgia
Zeta Beta Tau Fraternity House, University of Florida, Gainesville, Florida

1953 Brewer House, East Fishill, New York
Lee House, Midland, Michigan
Masieri Memorial Building, Grand Canal, Venice, Italy
Morris House II ("Seacliff"), San Francisco, California
Pieper and Montooth Office Building, Scottsdale, Arizona
Pointview Residences Apartment Tower, Pittsburgh
FM Radio Station, Jefferson, Wisconsin
Rhodedendron Chapel, Bear Run, Pennsylvania
Restaurant for Yosemite National Park, California

1954 Barnsdall Park Municipal Gallery, Los Angeles, California
Christian Science Reading Room, Riverside, Illinois

Tipshus Clinic, Stockton, California
Cornwell House, West Goshen, Pennsylvania
Freund Department Store, San Salvador,
    El Salvador
Rebhuhn House, Fort Meyers, Florida
Schwenn House, Verona, Wisconsin

1955 Adelman House, Whitefish Bay, Wisconsin
    Barton House, Downer's Grove, Illinois
    Blumberg House, Des Moines, Iowa
    Boswell House I, Cincinnati
    Christian Science Church, Bolinas, California
    Coats House, Hillsborough, California
    Cooke House, Virginia Beach, Virginia
        (Scheme II)
    Dlesk House, Manestee, Michigan
    Gillin House, Hollywood, California
    Jankowski House I, Oakland County,
        Michigan
    Lenkurt Electric Company Administration and
        Manufacturing Building, San Mateo,
        California
    Miller House, Milford, Michigan
    Morris Guest House, San Francisco,
        California
    Neuroseum (Hospital and Clinic), Madison,
        Wisconsin
    Oboler House II, Los Angeles, California
    "One Room House," Phoenix, Arizona
    Pieper House, Phoenix, Arizona
    Sussman House, Rye, New York
    Wieland Motel, Hagerstown, Maryland

1956 Boebel house, Boscobel, Wisconsin
    Bramlett Hotel, Mephis, Tennessee
    Golden Beacon skyscraper, Chicago, Illinois
    Gross House, Hackensack, New Jersey
    Hunt House, Scootsdale, Arizona
    Tonkens Loan Office, Cincinnati
    Mile High Skscraper, Chicago, Illinois
    Morris House ("Quietwater"), Stinson Beach,
        California
    Sports Pavilion, Belmont, Long Island,
        New York
    O'Keefe House, Santa Barbara, California
    Roberts House, Seattle, Washington
    Schuck House, South Hadley, Massachusetts
    Stillman House, Cornwall on Hudson,
        New York
    Vallarino Houses, Panama City, Panama

1957 Adams House, St. Paul, Minnesota
    Nezam Ameri Palace, Tehran, Iran
    Arizona State Capitol, Papago Park, Phoenix,
        Arizona
    Baghdad Cultural Center, Baghdad, Iraq
    University of Baghdad, Baghdad, Iraq
    Bimson House, Phoenix, Arizona
    Brooks House, Middleton, Wisconsin
    Hartman House, Lansing, Michigan
    Hennesy Houses (two projects), Smoke Rise,
        New Jersey
    Herberger House, Maricopa County, Arizona
    Highway Motel, Madison, Wisconsin
    Fisher Housing Project, Whiteville,
        North Carolina
    Hoyer House, Maricopa County, Arizona
    Juvenile Study Center Building B,
        University of Wichita, Kansas
    Gate Lodge for Fallingwater, Bear Run,
        Pennsylvania
    McKinney House, Cloquet, Minnesota
    Miller House, near Roxbury, Connecticut
    Mills House II, Princeton, New Jersey
    U.S. Rubber Company Model Exhibition
        Houses (exhibition project), New York
    Moreland House, Austin, Texas
    Postal Telegraph Building, Baghdad, Iraq
    Post Office, Spring Green, Wisconsin
    Schanbacher Store, Springfield, Illinois
    Shelton House, Long Isalnd, New York
    Sottil House, Cuernavaca, Mexico
    Stracke House, Appleton, Wisconsin
    Wedding Chapel for the Claremont Hotel,
        Berkeley, California
    Wilson House, Morgantown, North Carolina
    Zieger House, Grosse Isalnd, Michigan

1958 Leuchauer Clinic, Fresno, Claifornia
    Colgrove House, Hamilton, Ohio
    Crosby-Lambert House, Colbert County,
        Alabama
    Franklin House, Louisville, Kentucky
    Guttierez House, Albuquerque, New Mexico
    Hanley Airplane Hangar, Benton Harbor,
        Michigan
    Jones Chapel (Trinity Chapel), University of
        Oklahoma, Norman, Oklahoma
    Lagomarsino House, San Jose, California
    Libbey House, Grand Rapids, Michigan
    Lovness Cottages, Stillwater, Minnesota

    Mike Todd Universal Theater, Los Angeles,
        California
    Pre-Fab III and Pre-Fab IV for Marshall
        Erdman Associates, Madison, Wisconsin
    Spring Green Auditorium, Spring Green,
        Wisconsin
    Unity Chapel, Taliesin Valley, Spring Green,
        Wisconsin

1959 Art Gallery, Arizona State University, Tempe,
        Arizona
    Donohoe House, Phoenix, Arizona
    Furgatch House, San Diego, California
    Mann House, Putnam County, New York
    Penfield House II, Willoughby, Ohio
    Daniel Wieland House, Hagerstown,
        Maryland
    Gilbert Wieland House, Hagerstown,
        Maryland

3 Writings by Frank Lloyd Wright

Books

Ausgeführte Bauten und Entwerfe von Frank Lloyd Wright [Building Plans and Designs of Frank Lloyd Wright]; Ernst Wasmuth, Berlin, 1910.

Frank Lloyd Wright: Ausgeführte Bauten [Frank Lloyd Wright: Building Plans]; Ernst Wasmuth A.G., Berlin, 1911.

The Japanese Print: An Interpretation; The Ralph Fletcher Seymour Co., 1912 and revised and enlarged edition, Horizon Press, 1967.

Modern Architecture; Being the Kahn Lectures for 1930 Princeton University Press, 1931.

An Autobiography; Longmans, Green and Co., 1938. Revised and enlarged editions: Faber and Faber, 1945; Horizon Press, 1977.

The Disappearing City; William Fraquhar Payson, 1932.

Architecture and Modern Life (with Baker Brownell); Harper and Brothers, 1937.

An Organic Architecture: The Architecture of Democracy (transcript of four lectures given at the Royal Institute of British Architects in London); Lund Humphries and Co., 1939.

When Democracy Builds; University of Chicago
Press, 1945.

Genius and the Mobocracy; Duell, Sloan and
Pearce, 1929. Enlarged edition, Secker and
Warburg, 1972.

The Future of Architecture; Horizon Press, 1953.

The Natural House; Horizon Press, 1954.

*The Story of the Tower: The Tree That Escaped The
Crowded Forest*; Horizon Press, 1956.

A Testament; Horizon Press, 1957.

The Living City; Horizon Press, 1958.

Drawings for a Living Architecture; Horizon Press,
1959.

Catalogues and Pamphlets by Frank Lloyd Wright.

*Hiroshige: An Exhibition of Color prints from the
Collection of Frank Lloyd Wright*; The Art
Institute of Chicago, 1906.

*Antique Color Prints from the Collection of Frank
Lloyd Wright*; The Arts Club of Chicago
Exhibition, 1917.

Experimenting with Human Lives; The Ralph
Fletcher Seymour Co., 1923

*The Frank Lloyd Wright Collection of Japanese
Antique Prints* (Auction catalogue);
The Anderson galleries, New York, 1927.

Articles by Frank Lloyd Wright

"A Home in a Prairie Town," *Ladies' Home
Journal*; 18, No. 3, February 1901.

"The Art and Craft of the Machine," *Brush and
Pencil*; 8, No. 2, May 1901.

"A Small House with Lots of Room in It," *Ladies'
Home Journal*; 18, No. 8, July 1901.

"In The Cause of Architecture," *Architectural
Record*; 23, No. 3, March 1908.

"In The Cause of Architecture: Second Paper,"
Architectural Record; 35, No. 5, May 1914.

"In The Cause of Architecture: In the Wake of the
Quake; Concerning the Imperial Hotel,
Tokio: I," *Western Architect*; 32, No. 11,
November 1923. Part II: *Western Architect*;
33, No. 2, February 1924.

"Why the Japanese Earthquake Did Not Destroy
the Imperial Hotel," *Liberty*; 4, December 3,
1927.

"In The Cause of Architecture: I. The Logic of the
Plan," *Architectural Record*; 63, No. 1,
January 1928.

"In The Cause of Architecture: II. What 'Styles'

Mean to the Architect," *Architectural Record*;
63, No. 2, February 1928.

"In The Cause of Architecture: III. The Meaning of
Materials—Stone," *Architectural Record*; 63,
No. 4, April 1928.

"Broadacre City: A New Community Plan,"
Architectural Record; 77, No. 4, April 1935.

"Frank Lloyd Wright," *Architectural Forum*; 68,
No. 1, January 1938.

"*Life* Presents in Collaboration with the
Architectural Forum Eight Houses For
Modern Living Especially Designed by
Famous American Architects for Four
Representative Families Earning $2,000 to
$10,000 a Year,", *Life*, 5, September 26, 1938.

"Frank Lloyd Wright," *Architectural Forum*; 88,
No. 1, January 1948.

Collections of Wright's drawings, writings and talks

Drexler, Arthur, ed.; *The Drawings of Frank Lloyd
Wright*; Horizon Press, 1962.

Gutheim, Frederick, ed.; *Frank Lloyd Wright on
Architecture: Selected Writings, 1894-1940*;
Duell, Sloan and Pearce, 1941.

Gutheim, Frederick, ed.; I*n The Cause of
Architecture: Frank Lloyd Wright*;
Architectural Record and McGraw Hill,
1975.

Kaufmann, Edgar, ed.; *An American Architecture:
Frank Lloyd Wright*; Horizon Press, 1955.

Kaufmann, Edgar, and Raeburn, Ben, eds.; *Frank
Lloyd Wright: Writings and Buildings*;
Horizon Press, 1960.

Pfeiffer, Bruce Brooks, ed.; *Frank Lloyd Wright
Collected Writings 1894-1930*; Introduction
by Kenneth Frampton, Rizzoli, in association
with the Frank Lloyd Wright Foundation,
1992.

4 Selected Bibliography

Abernathy, Ann, and Thorpe, John; *The Oak Park
Home and Studio of Frank Lloyd Wright*;
Frank Lloyd Wright Home and Studio
Foundation, 1988.

Blake, Peter; *Frank Lloyd Wright: Architecture and
Space*; Penguin, 1964.

Brooks, H. Allen; *The Prairie School: Frank Lloyd
Wright and His Midwest Contemporaries*;
University of Toronto Press, 1972.

Connors, Joseph; *The Robie House of Frank Lloyd
Wright*; University of Chicago Press, 1984.

Costantino, Maria; *Frank Lloyd Wright*; Crescent
Books, 1991.

Costantino, Maria; *Frank Lloyd Wright Design*;
Brompton Books, 1995.

Gebhard, David, and Zimmerman, Scott (photographs); *Romanza: The California
Architecture of Frank Lloyd Wright*; Thames
and Hudson, 1989.

Gill, Brendan; *Many Masks: A Life of Frank Lloyd
Wright*; Heinemann, 1988.

Greene, Aaron G.; *An Architecture for Democracy:
The Marin County Civic Center*; Grendon
Publishing, 1990.

Hanks, David A.; *The Decorative Designs of Frank
Lloyd Wright*; Dutton, 1979.

Hanks, David A.; *Frank Lloyd Wright: preserving
and Architectural Heritage*; Decorative
Designs from The Domino's Pizza Collection,
Studio Vista, 1989.

Hanna, Paul R. and Jean S.; *Frank Lloyd Wright's
Hanna House*; Southern Illinois University
Press, 1987.

Hitchcock, Henry-Russell; I*n the Nature of
Materials: The Buildings of Frank Lloyd
Wright 1887-1941*; Da Capo Press, 1973.

Hoffman, Donald; *Frank Lloyd Wright's
Fallingwater: The House and Its History*;
Dover, 1978.

Hoffman, Donald; *Frank Lloyd Wright:
Architecture and Nature*; Dover, 1986.

Hoffman, Donald; *Frank Lloyd Wright's Hollyhock
House*; Dover, 1992.

Kaufmann, Edgar Jr.; *Fallingwater: A Frank Lloyd
Wright Country House*; The Architectural
Press, 1986.

Kaufmann, Edgar Jr.; *9 Commentaries on Frank
Lloyd Wright*; MIT Press, 1989.

Lipman, Jonathan; *Frank Lloyd Wright and the
Johnson Wax Buildings*; Rizzoli, 1986.

Lind, Carla; *The Wright Style*; Simon and Schuster,
1992.

Manson, Grant Carpenter; *Frank Lloyd Wright to
1910: The First Golden Age*; Reinhold
Publishing Corporation, 1958.

Pfeiffer, Bruce Brooks, ed.; *Letters to Clients: Frank

Lloyd Wright; California State University, 1986.

Quinan, Jack; *Frank Lloyd Wright's Larkin Building: Myth and Fact*; MIT Press, 1987.

Sanderson, Arlene, ed.; *Wright Sites: A Guide to Frank Lloyd Wright Public Places*; Princeton Architectural Press, 1995.

Scully, Vincent Jr; *Frank Lloyd Wright*; Masters of World Architecture Series, George Braziller, 1960.

Sergeant, John; *Frank Lloyd Wright's Usonian Houses: The Case for Organic Architecture*; Whitney Library of Design, 1984.

Smith, Kathryn; *Frank Lloyd Wright: Hollyhock House and Olive Hill*; Rizzoli, 1992.

Storrer, William; *The Architecture of Frank Lloyd Wright: A Complete Catalog*; MIT Press, 1979.

Storrer, William; *The Frank Lloyd Wright Companion*; University of Chicago Press, 1993.

Sweeny, Robert L.; *Wright in Hollywood: Visions of a New Architecture*; MIT Press, 1994.

Wright, Olgivanna; *Frank Lloyd Wright: His Life, His Work, His Words*; Horizon Press, 1961.

RIGHT: FRANK LLOYD WRIGHT 1869–1959. The simple marker of the final resting place at Taliesin West of America's greatest architect.

Index